THE DEAF LEGAL DILEMMA

Equality law is audist. Deaf communities around the world continue to encounter Deaf Legal Exclusion through legal frameworks that define them narrowly and restrict their rights.

The *Deaf Legal Dilemma: Challenging Equality Law* examines why these frameworks have not delivered equality in practice. It argues that the core issue is structural misrecognition: law protects deaf people only when they accept a definition based on disability. Sign language, culture and community are treated as secondary.

Drawing on doctrinal and socio-legal analysis of the Equality Act 2010, case law of the European Court of Human Rights, and the UN Convention on the Rights of Persons with Disabilities, the book critiques how equality law relies on narrow definitions of fairness. What appears to be inclusion is often a Deaf Legal Illusion: equality claimed in principle but absent in practice.

Formal, substantive and transformative precepts of equality and the Deaf Equality Concepts are explored, assessing their ability to reflect deaf people's experiences.

The book analyses five models used to categorise deaf people in law and policy: disability, language minority, culturo-linguistic community, ethnic group and Indigenous group. In response, the Deaf Rights Model is proposed, which brings the five models together as complementary rather than competing.

The *Deaf Legal Dilemma* establishes Deaf Legal Studies as a field grounded in the priorities and expertise of deaf communities. It invites lawmakers, practitioners and scholars to rethink the purpose of the law and the structures through which deaf people are recognised.

The Deaf Legal Dilemma

Challenging Equality Law

Rob Wilks

•HART•
OXFORD • LONDON • NEW YORK • NEW DELHI • SYDNEY

HART PUBLISHING
Bloomsbury Publishing Plc
Kemp House, Chawley Park, Cumnor Hill, Oxford, OX2 9PH, UK
1385 Broadway, New York, NY 10018, USA
Bloomsbury Publishing Ireland Limited, 29 Earlsfort Terrace, Dublin 2, D02 AY28, Ireland

HART PUBLISHING, the Hart/Stag logo, BLOOMSBURY and the Diana logo are trademarks of Bloomsbury Publishing Plc

First published in Great Britain 2026

1

A catalogue record for this book is available from the British Library.

A catalogue record for this book is available from the Library of Congress.

ISBN: HB: 978-1-50998-066-6
ePDF: 978-1-50998-064-2
ePub: 978-1-50998-065-9

Typeset by Amnet

For product safety related questions contact productsafety@bloomsbury.com

To find out more about our authors and books visit www.hartpublishing.co.uk. Here you will find extracts, author information, details of forthcoming events and the option to sign up for our newsletters.

For deaf communities globally,
this is for you.

CONTENTS

TABLE OF CASES

TABLE OF LEGISLATION

1

Deaf Realities

Forget everything you thought you knew about deaf people. This book will put things straight. Let us start with 'the problem'. Simply put, the problem is that equality law is not working for deaf people. In fact, I would go as far as to say that equality law is audist. The term 'audism' was coined by Humphries, who defines it as the belief that one is superior based on an ability to hear or behave like someone who can hear.[1] Eckert and Rowley describe audism as the differential treatment of individuals based on their hearing and communication abilities, influenced by societal assumptions and prejudices.[2] Bauman suggests that audism involves devaluing deaf individuals through stereotypes that portray them as incompetent and intellectually inferior.[3] In essence, audism refers to the belief held by hearing individuals, whether consciously or subconsciously, that they are superior to deaf individuals, resulting in differential treatment based on these thoughts, assumptions, prejudices, and stereotypes. Equality law is audist because it plays a role in labelling deaf individuals as disabled, disregarding deaf culture, and undervaluing the importance of sign language in deaf communities.

This book's focus on understanding and advocating for deaf individuals might raise questions about why we need specific attention compared to other disability groups. This is fair, particularly as society perceives deaf people as disabled first and foremost because they have lost a vital sense: hearing. As such, society's response to the existence of such disabled people – including deaf people – has generally been for government and the legislature to ensure that they are 'looked after',[4] predominantly through the social welfare system. Following the advancement of the disability rights movement in the 1980s and 1990s, however, the rights of disabled people were brought to the attention of Parliament and eventually resulted in the enactment of the Disability Discrimination Act 1995 (DDA 1995), which provided disabled people with protection from disability discrimination for the first time. Deaf people, of course, were involved in the disability rights movement, and so they too, found themselves falling within the auspices of the

[1] Tom Humphries, 'Communicating across Cultures (Deaf-Hearing) and Language Learning' (Doctoral Thesis, Union Institute and University, 1977).

[2] Richard Clark Eckert and Amy June Rowley, 'Audism: A Theory and Practice of Audiocentric Privilege' (2013) 37 *Humanity & Society* 101.

[3] H-Dirksen L Bauman, 'Audism: Exploring the Metaphysics of Oppression' (2004) 9 *Journal of Deaf Studies and Deaf Education* 239.

[4] Harlan Lane, *The Mask of Benevolence: Disabling the Deaf Community* (Alfred A Knopf, 1992).

DDA 1995. With the amalgamation of all anti-discrimination legislation into the Equality Act 2010 (EqA 2010), the status quo for deaf people continues.

Alongside developments in disability rights, not only in the UK but also at European and international level, the field of Deaf Studies took on a momentum of its own, and in particular, the 'deaf identity' has attracted significant attention. It gradually became clear – as deaf people continued to experience inequality – that being part of the disability rights movement was not garnering the desired results, with the stumbling block being that many deaf people with a deaf identity consider themselves to be part of a culturo-linguistic minority rather than disabled. Ultimately, when a deaf individual is in a group of disabled people, that deaf person is in a group of hearing people, and it is likely they will continue to experience the attitudinal and communication barriers associated with hearing people generally. Perhaps then, the 'deaf are disabled' ideology is doing more harm than good, or at the very least is reinforcing the status quo in how deaf people are to be treated by society. What would happen instead if we viewed deaf people as a culturo-linguistic minority, as a language minority, as an ethnic group, or as an Indigenous group? If we did, how effective would equality law at international, European and UK level be in addressing their inequalities? This is not, however, the full story. Yes, the central argument is that deaf people's language rights should be recognised alongside their disabled rights, but it is of course, not that simple.

Deaf communities are certainly not monolithic. Instead, they are multifaceted, multicultural, multi-racial, and comprised of individuals with diverse genders, sexualities, abilities, family structures, deaf+ identities, and lesbian, gay, bisexual, transgender, queer or questioning, intersex and other identities. They span generations, with experiences and perspectives differing between younger and older members. Deaf individuals have a variety of socioeconomic backgrounds which impact upon their access to resources and educational opportunities. Differing experiences are had depending on residence in a rural or urban area and the level of deaf community presence. How or why an individual is deaf often shapes their experiences. There are ongoing discussions about the most appropriate educational approaches for deaf children, with camps advocating for oralism (focusing on spoken language) versus a bilingual approach (using the national sign language and the monoglot language). Cochlear implants and other hearing technologies raise complex questions about identity and how deaf communities define themselves. First-wave deaf identity politics was the binary choice between the medical model and social model, usually manifest as the choice between oralism and sign language. We are currently in the second wave, whereby instead of a fixed state of identity, there is a multiplicity of identities which may coexist.[5] A principal aim of this book is to unpack the singular, monolithic view of deafness that pervades in legal frameworks and societal attitudes, which I argue hinders the effectiveness of equality law in achieving true equality[6] for deaf communities.

[5] Guy McIlroy and Claudine Storbeck, 'Development of Deaf Identity: An Ethnographic Study' (2011) 16 *Journal of Deaf Studies and Deaf Education* 494.

[6] What 'true equality' for deaf people looks like is explored in chs 2 and 4.

I. The Scale of Inequality

There are no two ways about it: equality law is failing deaf people. Deaf people continue to experience inequalities in many walks of life, from cradle to grave. When identified at birth or shortly thereafter as deaf, parents are expected to make decisions influenced by professionals whose main focus is on medical intervention, rehabilitation and acquisition of the monoglot spoken language despite the fact that that very language is inaccessible as it relies on the ability to hear.[7] The focus is therefore not to ensure the deaf child is able to acquire language(s) on their own terms and develop appropriate identities. Deaf children do not receive the education to which they are entitled[8] – this can also depend on their family's socioeconomic class[9] – and by the end of their mandatory education, have not fully developed the sufficient language skills or literacy to function and thrive in a monoglot-hearing-dominant world.[10]

In addition to language acquisition and education, childhood involves learning and socialisation, including the development of friendships and the acquisition of basic life skills. Adolescence is a time of physical and emotional changes, exploration of identity, and the beginning of more complex relationships. However, deaf children and young people do not always have the wherewithal to make friends and grow their social networks, as it does very much depend on how accommodating and accessible their families, education institutions and local communities are, and whether they are able to develop that all-important sense of belonging. With mainstreaming the norm, deaf children and young people are less likely to meet deaf peers, be part of deaf communities and develop deaf identities. Instead, they find themselves trying to fit in – sometimes desperately – within their hearing spheres, with varying degrees of success. Inevitably, they will at times feel that they do not quite belong anywhere.

During adulthood, deaf individuals will encounter a variety of experiences related to employment, health and the law. Many people spend a significant portion of their lives working, which can provide a sense of purpose and financial stability. Once they enter the world of work, however, deaf people experience inequalities due to the failures of the after-birth care and education system. They may not have the prerequisite qualifications to secure certain employment and develop careers, and also have to overcome societal barriers and attitudes towards deaf people.

[7] Rob Wilks and Rachel O'Neill, 'Deaf Education in Scotland and Wales: Attitudes to British Sign Language in Deaf Education Compared to Gaelic and Welsh' (2022), https://blogs.ed.ac.uk/deafeducation/wp-content/uploads/sites/5764/2022/10/2-FINAL-REPORT.pdf.

[8] Consortium for Research in Deaf Education, '2022 UK-Wide Summary' (National Deaf Children's Society, 2022), www.ndcs.org.uk/media/8489/cride-2022-uk-report-final.pdf.

[9] Rachel O'Neill and others, 'Families Living on a Low Income Bringing up Deaf Children' (2019), www.ssc.education.ed.ac.uk/research/tellingit/tellingit_final.pdf.

[10] Kate Rowley, 'Language Acquisition: Bimodal and Bilingual' (BDA BSL Conference, London, 17 March 2023), https://vimeo.com/812803921; National Deaf Children's Society, 'Deaf Pupils Achieve an Entire GCSE Grade Less for Sixth Year Running' (9 August 2021), www.ndcs.org.uk/about-us/news-and-media/latest-news/deaf-pupils-achieve-an-entire-gcse-grade-less-for-sixth-year-running.

They also experience difficulties in accessing the job market and during recruitment, and face issues such as discrimination, harassment and unfair treatment in the workplace and in promotion opportunities.[11] The employment opportunities afforded to deaf people throughout their adulthood will in turn determine the quality of their twilight years.

While many deaf individuals enjoy good physical and mental health, others may face chronic illnesses, injuries, or mental health conditions that require ongoing management. Access to healthcare, including preventative services and treatment options, can play a crucial role in maintaining overall well-being. However, deaf people generally do not have equal access to such services. They encounter difficulties in accessing healthcare and communicating with healthcare professionals, resulting in poorer health outcomes.[12] They also face challenges in seeking assistance, potentially overlooking life-threatening conditions, and receiving substandard treatment upon diagnosis.[13] A research study within audiology services revealed disempowerment and a lack of autonomy among deaf individuals, highlighting the necessity for a culturally sensitive and customised service.[14] This issue extends further into the realm of mental health, where deaf individuals are twice as likely to confront mental health difficulties compared to their hearing counterparts due to the absence of accessible and culturally sensitive mental health services.[15]

In addition, as deaf people age and their care needs increase, they are likely to find themselves part of a care system that forgets their unique needs and isolates them from their deaf community as they near the end of their lives. The elderly generation of deaf individuals face various challenges in terms of their physical well-being, access to resources, and personal safety due to the societal, educational, and economic circumstances in which they were raised. It is essential for

[11] Laura Arrowsmith, 'Hidden Disadvantage' (2013), https://rnid.org.uk/wp-content/uploads/2020/05/Hidden-Disadvantage-full-report.pdf; Sarah CE Batterbury-Magill, 'The Legal Status of BSL and ISL' (2014), https://bda.org.uk/wp-content/uploads/2017/03/BDA_Legal-status-of-BSL-ISL_11-Mar-2014.pdf; Totaljobs, 'Deaf Jobseeker and Employee Experiences Survey' (2016), www.121captions.com/wp-content/uploads/2017/08/Deaf-jobseeker-and-employee-experiences-survey-report-2016.pdf; Lynne Barnes, 'Employment and Employability: The Experiences and Perceptions of Deaf Graduates' (Doctoral Thesis, University of Central Lancashire, 2017); Action on Hearing Loss, 'Working for Change 2018: Workplace Experiences - Survey Results' (2018); Royal Association for Deaf People, 'Deaf Advance: Deaf People, Employment and Career Progression' (Royal Association for Deaf People, 2021) 202.

[12] Alan Emond and others, 'Access to Primary Care Affects the Health of Deaf People.' (2015) 65 *The British journal of general practice: the journal of the Royal College of General Practitioners* 95; Alan Emond and others, 'The Current Health of the Signing Deaf Community in the UK Compared with the General Population: A Cross-Sectional Study' (2015) 5 *BMJ Open* 1.

[13] Royal National Institute for Deaf People and SignHealth, 'Still Ignored: The Fight for Accessible Healthcare - 2025 Research Report' (2025), https://signhealth.org.uk/wp-content/uploads/2025/04/ENGLAND-Still-Ignored-The-fight-for-Accessible-Healthcare-RESEARCH-report-FINAL.pdf; SignHealth, 'How the Health Service Is Failing Deaf People' (SignHealth, 2014).

[14] Celia Hulme, Alys Young and Kevin J Munro, 'Exploring the Lived Experiences of British Sign Language (BSL) Users Who Access NHS Adult Hearing Aid Clinics: An Interpretative Phenomenological Analysis' (2022) 61 *International Journal of Audiology* 744.

[15] Julia Terry and others, 'Deaf People Wales: Hidden Inequality' (2021), www.swansea.ac.uk/media/Deaf-People-Wales_Hidden-Inequality-2021.pdf.

their overall health and well-being to maintain social and cultural connections.[16] The current provision of residential care for deaf individuals is insufficient, failing to meet the needs of older deaf individuals and negatively impacting their quality of life.[17]

If deaf people run afoul of the law, they will experience an inaccessible criminal justice system, from arrest to trial and sentencing, in terms of how the authorities and court systems deal with them.[18] In prisons, they will experience a 'double sentence' due to the loneliness of being incarcerated with other inmates and staff not able to communicate with them.[19] They may also encounter legal issues related to their personal or professional lives, which may include disputes with employers, divorce and custody proceedings, conveyancing matters, wills and probate. Understanding and navigating the legal system can be complex and challenging, requiring the assistance of legal professionals, but it is well documented that deaf people lack access to legal advice,[20] compounding the issues.

In politics and public life, there is a conspicuous absence of deaf individuals representing their local communities at both local and national levels. This is further compounded by the dearth of support from political parties in addressing barriers and the financial burdens associated with running for elected office.[21]

[16] Alys Young, 'Older Deaf People and Social Care: A Review' (Royal Association for Deaf People and [sonus] 2014), https://research.manchester.ac.uk/files/67726760/POST-PEER-REVIEW-PUBLISHERS.PDF.

[17] Ros Hunt, Rosemary Oram and Alys Young, 'Older People Who Use BSL – Preferences for Residential Care Provision in Wales' (University of Manchester, 2010), https://apps.mhs.manchester.ac.uk/uploads/ProjectProfilesFiles/2184/OlderPeopleWalesOctoberFinalrevised.pdf.

[18] Mary Brennan and Richard Brown, *Equality before the Law: Deaf People's Access to Justice* (Douglas McLean, 1997); Frank Harrington and Graham H Turner, *Interpreting Interpreting: Studies and Reflections on Sign Language Interpreting* (Douglas McLean, 2000).

[19] Laura Kelly, 'Suffering in Silence: The Unmet Needs of d/Deaf Prisoners' [2017] *Prison Service Journal* 3; Laura Margaret Kelly, 'Sounding out d/Deafness: The Experiences of d/Deaf Prisoners' (2017) 8 *Journal of Criminal Psychology* 20; Laura Kelly-Corless and Daniel McCulloch, 'Why Deaf Prisoners Have Been in a State of Lockdown since Well before COVID-19' (*The Conversation*, 13 April 2021), https://theconversation.com/why-deaf-prisoners-have-been-in-a-state-of-lockdown-since-well-before-covid-19-158173; Daniel McCulloch, 'Not Hearing Us: An Exploration of the Experience of Deaf Prisoners in English and Welsh Prisons' (Howard League for Penal Reform, 2012), http://oro.open.ac.uk/42456.

[20] John Borland and others, 'Responding to Discrimination: The Geography and Geometry of Advice Provision in England, Scotland and Wales' (Equality and Human Rights Commission, 2009); Jim Kyle, Hilary Sutherland and S Stockley, 'Legal Choice - Silent Process: Engaging Legal Services When You Do Not Hear' (Deaf Studies Trust, 2012).

[21] Elizabeth Evans and Stefanie Reher, 'Barriers to Elected Office for Disabled People' (Government Equalities Office 2021), www.gov.uk/government/publications/barriers-to-elected-office-for-disabled-people/barriers-to-elected-office-for-disabled-people; Elizabeth Evans and Stefanie Reher, 'Disability and Political Representation: Analysing the Obstacles to Elected Office in the UK' (2022) 43 *International Political Science Review* 697; John Pring, 'Government Faces Legal Action over Election Access Fund' (*Disability News Service*, 12 April 2018), www.disabilitynewsservice.com/government-faces-legal-action-over-election-access-fund; Liam O'Dell, 'Deaf News: Deaf Local Election Candidate "Denied" Interpreter Funding by Government' (*Limping Chicken*, 16 April 2021), https://limpingchicken.com/2021/04/16/deaf-news-deaf-local-election-candidate-denied-interpreter-funding-by-government; UK Parliament, 'Chapter 12: Participation in Politics' (*Select Committee on the Equality Act 2010 and Disability The Equality Act 2010: the impact on disabled people*, 24 March 2016), https://publications.parliament.uk/pa/ld201516/ldselect/ldeqact/117/11715.htm.

From the perspective of the electorate, political information is generally limited,[22] and a survey revealed that deaf citizens were unable to exert influence over their own country's political system and lacked a comprehensive understanding of their national parties' ideologies.[23] Ensuring the participation of deaf individuals in politics is an important objective, and Emery acknowledges that their ability to engage in political action and establish connections with government representatives contributes to their experience as equal citizens.[24]

The evidence of deaf people's inequality is clearly overwhelming. What is particularly perplexing is why deaf people continue to experience inequality despite the equality and anti-discrimination laws that were designed to protect them from such treatment. The equality instruments relevant to deaf communities in the UK are the Universal Declaration of Human Rights ('the Human Rights Declaration'), the European Convention on Human Rights ('the Human Rights Convention'), the Equality Act 2010 (EqA 2010) and the United Nations Convention on the Rights of Persons with Disabilities ('the Disability Convention'). The Human Rights Declaration and Convention date from 1948 and 1950 respectively and were ratified in response to the atrocities of World War Two, particularly the persecution of the Jewish people and others during the Holocaust. The Declaration declares that all human beings have 'equal and inalienable rights' before the law and protection from discrimination, Article 14 of the Human Rights Convention states that all humans have a right to protection from discrimination, and the EqA 2010 affords those with a protected characteristic with recourse if they experience discrimination in the workplace, in goods and services, and in further and higher education, classified as either direct and indirect discrimination, harassment, discrimination arising in consequence of disability or the failure to make reasonable adjustments. Finally, the Disability Convention reaffirms that the rights contained within the Declaration and other UN conventions and declarations that persons with disabilities can expect protection from discrimination. Deaf people are of course human beings, and as such, can expect the same protections as everyone else.

At first glance, these equality instruments clearly should be dealing with deaf people's inequalities. The Human Rights Declaration and Convention have been around since the 1950s, and while the EqA 2010 is 'new' in relative terms, its predecessor, the DDA 1995 has been on the statute books since the late 1990s, and the Disability Convention was ratified in 2007, more than 18 years ago at the time of writing. The examples outlined of deaf people's inequalities are all fairly recent, with the oldest source cited from 1997. Surely there should have been an improvement since then. Surely some of the inequalities deaf people experience should

[22] Gill Valentine and Tracey Skelton, '"An Umbilical Cord to the World": The Role of the Internet in D/Deaf People's Information and Communication Practices' (2009) 12 *Information, Communication & Society* 44.

[23] Annika Pabsch, 'Lessons from the 2013 EUD UNCRPD Survey' in Annika Pabsch (ed), *Article 29: Participation in Political and Public Life* (European Union of the Deaf, 2014).

[24] Steven D Emery, 'Citizenship and the Deaf Community' (Doctoral dissertation, University of Central Lancashire, 2006).

have been eradicated by now. It is clear that there is still long way to go, so what is the hold-up? Why is it taking so long? Why are we not seeing results yet? These are the questions that this book aims to address.

II. The Deaf Legal Dilemma

Equality law generally does not provide protections for all aspects of a deaf individual's identity. The main reason for this, I argue, is because the framing of deaf people as disabled is problematic, giving rise to what is termed the Deaf Legal Dilemma, whereby deaf people are faced with a stark choice: accept the disability label, or have no access to any rights at all. On one hand, deaf individuals should not be discriminated against simply due to being deaf. On the other, viewing deafness solely as a disability might ignore the unique cultural aspects and linguistic needs of deaf communities. I refer to this as the 'deaf-disabled' and 'language minority' dichotomy,[25] and it is also referred to as 'dual category status'[26] or the Deaf Duality Paradox.[27] Deaf-disabled rights are generally recognised and afford protections and benefits if deaf people accept that classification. Language minority rights do also exist, usually in the form of sign language law, but generally these do not proffer the same level of protection or benefits as deaf-disabled rights. The Deaf Legal Dilemma is a concept that has several layers, and is explored in detail in chapter four. In particular, deaf-disabled rights are explored in relation to the medical/individual, social, minority group, cultural, and human rights models of disability, whereas language minority rights are considered in the context of deaf people as a culturo-linguistic group, an ethnic group, and an Indigenous group.

So, the aim of this exercise is to examine the tension between these two types of deaf rights. I will explore how the different disability models influence the rights afforded when viewed as disabled, and how recognising deaf communities as linguistic and cultural groups can shape protections related to sign language and cultural identity. Currently, the Deaf Legal Dilemma is framed as a binary choice, but a more comprehensive approach is needed that sees these rights as complementary. Recognising the reality that deafness can be both a disability and a cultural identity, I advocate for a combination of deaf-disabled and language minority rights. This approach has the potential to significantly reduce, if not eradicate, the inequalities faced by deaf people and their communities.

The Deaf Legal Dilemma poses a significant challenge for law- and policymakers to address, but it is not the only obstacle preventing equality law from

[25] Rob Wilks, 'Developing Deaf Jurisprudence: The Role of Interpreters and Translators' in Christopher Stone and others (eds), *Routledge Handbook of Sign Language Translation and Interpreting* (Routledge, 2022).

[26] Maartje De Meulder and Joseph J Murray, 'Buttering Their Bread on Both Sides?' (2017) 41 *Language Problems and Language Planning* 136, 139.

[27] Alexandre Bloxs, 'The Deaf Duality Paradox as a Trait of the Deaf Legal Theory' in Rob Wilks and Dai O'Brien (eds), *Developing Deaf Legal Theory* (in preparation).

fully protecting deaf people. Several additional issues, explored below, complement our understanding of the dilemma. As you progress through the book, consider these factors alongside the Deaf Legal Dilemma to gain a comprehensive picture of the challenges faced by deaf people, and by the actors who can do something about it. I refer to these as factors, patterns or common denominators throughout.

III. Charity and the Patriarchy

Society typically functions under the assumption that it must provide support and care for deaf individuals for them to live their lives to the fullest, which begins with the assumption that deaf people need 'help'. The treatment of deaf people lies in a state that invokes charity, where society seeks to do good and reaffirm its moral conscience.[28] While Mor argues that this is due to the structure of the market economy and negative social attitudes,[29] others go as far as to suggest that the aim is to divide society into distinct groups by establishing categories and drawing boundaries between what is considered normal and abnormal, competent and incompetent, and able-bodied and disabled.[30] To put it more bluntly, ensuring that the out groups,[31] including deaf people and their communities, 'know their place'.

Lane suggests that society demonstrates paternalistic tendencies towards deaf individuals in four ways. Firstly, hearing culture is imposed on deaf people without their consent. This is seen in the medicalisation of deafness and the practice of forced oralism.[32] Secondly, paternalistic authority describes deaf people differently from how they identify themselves, perpetuating negative stereotypes. Lane also highlights the 'White Man's Burden test', where benefactors feel responsible for providing language and culture to deaf people, exemplified by the emphasis on cochlear implants without considering individual needs. Lastly, paternalistic relations are influenced by economic motivations, with deaf individuals becoming consumers of hearing-related technology regulated by hearing companies. This can influence policy decisions in favour of these technologies over sign language.[33]

This paternalistic approach not only fails to empower deaf communities but also reinforces a hierarchy that undermines the legitimacy of the deaf identity and cultural practices. Moving forward, we need to dismantle these unequal power dynamics and advocate for policies that centre deaf self-determination.

[28] Harlan Lane, *The Mask of Benevolence: Disabling the Deaf Community* (Alfred A Knopf, 1992).

[29] Sagit Mor, 'Between Charity, Welfare, and Warfare: A Disability Legal Studies Analysis of Privilege and Neglect in Israeli Disability Policy' (2006) 18 *Yale Journal of Law & the Humanities* 63, 71.

[30] Aart Hendriks and Theresia Degener, 'The Evolution of a European Perspective on Disability Legislation' (1994) 1 *European Journal of Health Law* 343, 348; Martha Minow, *Making All the Difference: Inclusion, Exclusion, and American Law* (Cornell University Press, 1990) 21–22.

[31] Henri Tajfel, 'Experiments in Intergroup Discrimination' (1970) 223 *Scientific American* 96.

[32] Blind, &c. Commission, 'Report of the Royal Commission on the Blind, the Deaf and Dumb Etc' (HM Stationery Office, 1889) C.-5781.

[33] Lane (n 4).

IV. Colonialism

Ladd asserts that deaf communities have undergone colonisation.[34] His examination of deaf cultures reveals that they are not only directly impacted by hearing culture, but also influenced by both compliance with and resistance against cultural domination.[35] In other words, the coloniser's culture is imposed on the colonised without their consent.[36] Colonialism is an association between multiple groups with unequal power, in which one group not only exercises control and governance over the other, but also strives to impose its culture onto the subordinate group.[37] According to Gartrell, colonialism is formal political control through an administrative system, accompanied by an ideology that justifies such control, which tends to perceive and treat the subordinate group as inherently 'different and inferior'.[38]

By recognising the deaf experience through a colonial lens, we again need to dismantle these unequal power dynamics and advocate for legal frameworks that respect deaf self-determination. Further research is needed to explore the historical and ongoing impacts of colonialism on deaf communities around the world. This research can inform advocacy efforts aimed at decolonising educational practices and dismantling power structures that disadvantage deaf individuals.

V. Cultural Competence

Service providers, employers, and law- and policymakers clearly lack cultural competence in working with deaf individuals. This lack of understanding can lead to ineffective communication, inappropriate adjustments, and discriminatory practices that undermine the intent of equality law. This lack of cultural competence has been discussed in the context of social and health care, with Orr and others[39] stating: 'Without a sophisticated knowledge of such cultural manifestations, no [one] can make a good . . . assessment of a . . . deaf person.'[40] The same applies to actors who lack cultural competence: without knowing or understanding the nuances associated with the deaf identity and culture, can they ever really provide services or employment, or to legislate, taking account of the deaf perspective?

The lack of cultural competence within service providers and lawmakers creates significant barriers for deaf people. To bridge this gap, educational initiatives

[34] Paddy Ladd, *Understanding Deaf Culture: In Search of Deafhood* (Multilingual Matters, 2003).

[35] ibid.

[36] Lane (n 4).

[37] Sally Engle Merry, 'Law and Colonialism' (1991) 25 *Law and Society Review* 889; Ladd (n 34) 79.

[38] Beverley Gartrell, 'Colonial Wives: Villains or Victims?' in Shirley Ardener and Hilary Callan (eds), *The Incorporated Wife* (Croom Helm, 1984) 4.

[39] F Orr, A DeMatteo, B Heller, M Lee, & M Nguyen, 'Psychological Assessment' in H Elliott, LE Glass, and JW Evans (eds), *Mental health assessment of deaf clients: A practical manual* (College Hill Press, 1987) 93-106 https://cir.nii.ac.jp/crid/1971993809809163826.

[40] Laura L Myers and Bruce A Thyer, 'Social Work Practice with Deaf Clients: Issues in Culturally Competent Assessment' (1997) 26 *Social Work in Health Care* 61.

promoting deaf culture and language fluency are essential. Additionally, shifting the perspective on deafhood as a cultural identity, not just a disability, can foster a more inclusive environment.

VI. Unconscious Bias

Unconscious bias is also prevalent in society and influences how actors interact with deaf people, and equality law is simply not able to address such attitudinal challenges. Unconscious bias is those automatic judgements our brains make when coming across individuals who may be different in some way. It is influenced by our individual backgrounds, personal experiences and societal stereotypes that we may hold to understand our social hierarchies and interact with other people.[41] It is clearly present when individuals in society at large – hearing people – meet deaf people.

Hearing individuals automatically make judgements about deaf people, and these judgements range from thinking that deaf people are stupid, that they are incapable of language and learning, that they need help to function in society, and that their 'hearing impairments' need curing so that they can live 'normal' lives. As Humphries puts it, deaf people are regarded by hearing people as 'languageless, speechless, unhearing, cultureless, and *strange*' (emphasis added).[42] In theory, equality law deals with situations where unconscious bias spills over into discriminatory acts against deaf people, but because it generally does not deal directly with unconscious bias, issues continue to persist. To be fair, unconscious bias is so rooted in our society and part of everyone's psyche that it is not something that can be eradicated all that easily. A solution to this issue is discussed in chapter two in the form of transformative equality. While legal frameworks alone cannot eradicate unconscious bias, they can be designed to mitigate its effects.

VII. Deaf Communities in Decline?

The deaf club holds significant importance, not only functioning as a repository of history and time but also serving as a central space that strengthens the social connections of deaf communities. This stability provided by the deaf club allows individuals in need to easily locate and access the community, including deaf individuals from hearing families and those seeking to fully immerse themselves in deaf culture and language.[43] According to Hadjikakou and Nikolaraizi, deaf clubs play a crucial role in safeguarding deaf culture and heritage, ensuring its

[41] Mihal Emberton, 'Unconscious Bias Is a Human Condition' (2021) 25 *The Permanente Journal* 1.

[42] Tom Humphries, 'Of Deaf-Mutes, the Strange, and the Modern Deaf Self' in Michael Harvey and Neil Glickman (eds), *Culturally Affirming Psychotherapy with Deaf Persons* (Lawrence Erlbaum Associates, 1996) 101.

[43] Dai O'Brien, Lisa Stead and Nicholas Nourse, 'Bristol Deaf Memories: Archives, Nostalgia and the Loss of Community Space in the Deaf Community in Bristol' (2019) 20 *Social & Cultural Geography* 899.

preservation and transmission to future generations, and serving as invaluable role models for young deaf children and their families, nurturing their sense of identity and belonging.[44]

Nonetheless, deaf clubs are in decline. In the UK at least, this can be attributed to various factors. Austerity measures have led to reduced funding for deaf clubs and deaf centres, thus impacting their availability.[45] Additionally, there is a generational decline in participation, with younger generations not stepping up to replace the older members who were traditionally associated with deaf clubs. In the past, deaf clubs served as important hubs for accessing information, initially through missionaries and later through social workers.[46] Moreover, these clubs facilitated knowledge exchange among members and provided opportunities for language acquisition.[47] Unfortunately, the transfer of knowledge and experiences from older generations to younger ones is not feasible in the current scenario.[48] Further, the progression of technology has caused a shift towards online interactions away from deaf clubs,[49] a fact not unnoticed by elderly deaf club members, who have expressed their dissatisfaction with the intrusion of technology into their lives, linking it to the fragmentation of their community.[50]

The decline of deaf clubs underscores the importance of fostering intergenerational connections and exploring alternative models for strengthening deaf communities, particularly in the digital age.

VIII. Education

Beyond what has been discussed so far, still deeper societal issues are woven throughout this book. One stark reality is the glaring disparity in education for deaf individuals, often hindered by mainstreaming policies, inadequate resources and a lack of qualified teachers of deaf children who understand and are willing to address head-on the challenges deaf children face rather than focusing on traditional methods that do not always work. This educational gap leaves many lagging behind their hearing peers, impacting their future opportunities and contributing

[44] Kika Hadjikakou and Magda Nikolaraizi, 'Deaf Clubs Today: Do They Still Have a Role to Play? The Cases of Cyprus and Greece' (2011) 155 *American Annals of the Deaf* 605.

[45] O'Brien, Stead and Nourse (n 43); Charlie Swinbourne, 'Bristol's Deaf Community Feel under Siege' (*The Guardian*, 15 September 2011), www.theguardian.com/commentisfree/2011/sep/15/bristol-deaf-centre-funding-cuts.

[46] Kate Attfield, 'The Deaf Collective: Opposition, Organisation and Difference' (Cardiff University, 2013).

[47] Alison Bryan and Steve Emery, 'The Case for Deaf Legal Theory Through the Eyes of Deaf Gain' in Joseph J Murray, H-Dirksen L Bauman (eds), *Deaf Gain: Raising the Stakes for Human Diversity* (University of Minnesota Press, 2014).

[48] Regan Thibodeau, 'Dynamics of Deaf Leadership: A Theoretical Model' (Doctoral dissertation, University of Southern Maine, 2019).

[49] Helen Blom and others, 'Finding Friends Online: Online Activities by Deaf Students and Their Well-Being' (2014) 9 *PLoS ONE* e88351; Michella Maiorana-Basas and Claudia M Pagliaro, 'Technology Use Among Adults Who Are Deaf and Hard of Hearing: A National Survey' (2014) 19 *The Journal of Deaf Studies and Deaf Education* 400.

[50] O'Brien, Stead and Nourse (n 43).

to wider inequalities. Further exacerbating this challenge is the societal misperception that early exposure to sign language hinders spoken language development, despite its proven benefits in cognitive and literacy skills. This lack of understanding creates a barrier to crucial language acquisition during the critical early years, perpetuating the educational disparity.

Addressing the educational disparities faced by deaf children requires a shift away from mainstreaming policies as well as a recognition of sign language as a fundamental right and a vital tool for cognitive development. Policymakers and educators must work collaboratively to develop and implement inclusive educational models that prioritise deaf children's language development and cultural identity. Investment in professional development programmes for teachers to enhance their sign language fluency and understanding of deaf pedagogy is crucial.

IX. Information, Communication and Access

The information, communication and access concept is particularly useful: deaf people generally do not have access to information and services, also known as incidental learning[51] or informal or unintentional learning,[52] because the journey to adulthood does not include the learning that takes place by listening and hearing what goes on around them, in conversations with family and friends, on the radio and other media, in public places, and in educational settings. Much incidental learning takes place in those environments, but for obvious reasons, deaf people do not have access to that information. Emery argues that this access is vital to citizenship as it enables social cohesion,[53] particularly as communication between deaf and hearing people is often fraught with problems. This concept is further explored in the context of legal advice with acquisition of information requiring prior knowledge to comprehend and understand that information.[54] Prior knowledge allows deaf people to receive and understand the advice given and take the necessary action. If, however, they do not have prior knowledge, then the whole process of acquiring information and moving forward armed with that information will simply not happen.

A more nuanced understanding of 'access' that considers the limitations of sign language interpreting and the importance of incidental learning is crucial for ensuring equal participation for deaf people in society. However, even the idea of 'access' is problematic, as society has not really grasped the concept of 'access' for deaf people.

[51] Michael M McKee and Peter C Hauser, 'Juggling Two Worlds' in Donald F Moores and Peter V Paul (eds), *Deaf Epistemologies: Multiple Perspectives on the Acquisition of Knowledge* (Gallaudet University Press, 2012).

[52] Karen Watkins and Victoria J Marsick, *Informal and Incidental Learning in the Workplace* (Routledge, 1990).

[53] Emery (n 24).

[54] Rob Wilks and Jeff Brattan-Wilson, 'Making the Law Work for Young Deaf People' (Royal Association for Deaf people, 2012).

Indeed, it is still a concept that has different layers not widely understood by deaf people themselves. Access is defined as the 'ability to derive benefits from things'.[55] Within this context, this means giving deaf people the ability to attend meetings, training courses and conferences, appointments with health professionals, go to work, travel, obtain legal advice and engage with public services. The usual type of 'access' is the provision of sign language interpreting services, and it is argued that such provision has become a 'quick fix to solve complex language issues', produces an 'illusion of inclusion',[56] and has become an 'institutionally normative' solution.[57] Public representation and interpreting at public events have become a symbol for 'inclusion' and 'access',[58] and can give the impression that deaf people are participating on equal terms. However, this is not always the case. Sign language interpreters can limit deaf people's access to information and create a dynamic where the interpreter controls the flow of communication, and the fact that the presence of a third party can change dynamics and affect trust and confidentiality is often ignored.[59] There is an alternative way of doing things: by providing 'language-concordant'[60] services, that is, monolingual services whereby a service is delivered in sign language.[61]

While sign language interpreting services remain an essential tool for communication, a more nuanced understanding of 'access' is crucial. Beyond physical access to spaces, deaf individuals require equal opportunity to acquire incidental learning and participate meaningfully in social interactions. This necessitates a two-pronged approach. Firstly, promoting the use of language-concordant services, delivered entirely in sign language, to empower deaf communities and foster a sense of ownership over information. Secondly, dismantling societal barriers that perpetuate the illusion of inclusion through interpreting alone is vital. By prioritising deaf-centric solutions and recognising the limitations of interpreting, we can move towards a society where deaf individuals have full access to information, fostering their active participation and enriching the social fabric of their and others' lives.

X. Intersectionality

Wu and Grant explain that each of us is distinct while also sharing experiences and traits with certain others in a specific group, and that it takes time for individuals to go through development processes individually and to fully understand

[55] Jesse C Ribot and Nancy Lee Peluso, 'A Theory of Access' (2003) 68 *Rural Sociology* 153.

[56] Maartje De Meulder and Hilde Haualand, 'Sign Language Interpreting Services: A Quick Fix for Inclusion?' (2019) 16 *Translation and Interpreting Studies* 19.

[57] Maartje De Meulder and Hilde Haualand, 'Sign Language Interpreting Services: A Quick Fix for Inclusion?' (World Association of Sign Language Interpreters Conference, Paris, France, 15 July 2019).

[58] Octavian Robinson, 'Puppets, Jesters, Memes, and Benevolence Porn: The Spectacle of Access' [2022] *Przegląd Kulturoznawczy* 329.

[59] Patricia d'Ardenne and others, 'Does Interpreter-Mediated CBT with Traumatized Refugee People Work? A Comparison of Patient Outcomes in East London' (2007) 35 *Behavioural and Cognitive Psychotherapy* 293.

[60] De Meulder and Haualand (n 57).

[61] Wilks (n 26) 258.

and integrate their cultural identities.[62] The deaf identity will intersect with other marginalised identities such as race, gender, sexual orientation, and disability, often compounding the disadvantages faced and highlighting the need for multi-faceted solutions.

Equality law needs to be intersectional in its approach to acknowledge the compounded disadvantages faced by deaf people with additional marginalised identities. Deaf women, for example, may face a unique set of challenges due to the intersection of sexism, audism, and other identity markers. Recognising these intersections is crucial for crafting effective legal and social solutions.

XI. Structure of the Book

So, where do we go from here? The barriers facing deaf people are clearly due to a multifaceted, complex myriad of circumstances and issues that are in themselves subject to considerable debate and controversy. If we return to the premise of this book, which is to understand the Deaf Legal Dilemma - the choice between being labelled disabled or having no rights at all - and challenging equality law, my proposal is that law should take into account the disability, language minority, culturo-linguistic, ethnic and Indigenous models that can be applied to deaf individuals. To ensure that deaf people have 'equal and inalienable rights' in parity with their hearing counterparts, they should be afforded rights that encapsulate the multifaceted nature of what it means to be deaf. This would in turn ensure that all or most of their identities are protected.

To that end, the aim of this book is to provide a comprehensive understanding of the legal rights and challenges faced by deaf communities. This chapter introduces the scope of the book and highlights 'the problem' by setting out the challenges faced by deaf people in education, employment, criminal justice, legal services, and their treatment in prisons and health settings in order to provide an understanding of the barriers deaf people continue to experience.

Chapter two will provide an overview of formal, substantive and transformative equality, a specific methodology that allows the author to categorise concepts of equality, thus establishing a standard of measurement by which it is possible to determine how effective particular concepts of equality are in eradicating inequality.

Chapter three will focus on equality law as it applies to deaf people, with particular attention paid to anti-discrimination law such as the Human Rights Declaration, the Human Rights Convention, the EqA 2010 and the Disability Convention. Relevant case law and communications under these provisions will

[62] Cheryl L Wu and Nancy C Grant, 'Intersectionality—Beyond the Individual: A Look Into Cultural Identity Development of Deaf and Hard-of-Hearing Children of Multicultural "Hearing" Families' in Irene W Leigh and Catherine A O'Brien (eds), *Deaf Identities: Exploring New Frontiers* (Oxford University Press, 2019) 226–27.

be outlined. Chapter four will consider the Deaf Legal Dilemma, focusing on the different models that can be applied to deaf people, and aim to synthesise a new deaf model – what I refer to as the Deaf Rights Model. Chapter five will focus on the Deaf Equality Concepts and how they apply to deaf people and their communities. Lastly, chapter six will provide a conclusion, summarising the key points covered in preceding chapters regarding the legal rights and challenges faced by deaf communities and how equality law can (or is not able to) address these issues.

XII. Closing Remarks

To bring this introductory chapter to a close, the aim of this work is to bridge the gap between the study of the law as it relates to deaf people, which has never before been attempted on this scale. This will contribute to the body of knowledge in legal studies, Deaf Studies and language policy, and trigger a new field of study to be known as Deaf Legal Studies.[63] The hope is this exposé of equality law as it relates to deaf people will equip the reader with a better understanding of the difficulties inherent in the law and what is needed to ensure deaf people have 'equal and inalienable rights' on par with their hearing peers.

[63] Rob Wilks, 'Special Section: Introducing Deaf Legal Studies - Editorial' (2026) 7(2) *Amicus Curiae*.

2

Framing Equality

What does it mean to achieve equality? Indeed, how does one know if equality has been achieved, if one does not know what equality is, and how to achieve it? I'm not the only one who has pondered this question. Given that the right to equality before the law is guaranteed by most constitutions around the world and equality as a concept touches every aspect of society, its meaning remains elusive,[1] to the extent that it has been called an 'empty idea'.[2] It has sparked debate across disciplines, societies, and legal systems for many years. As one would expect, that debate has generated a wealth of literature with scholars and writers attempting to define and interpret the term. This chapter aims to distil these debates, exploring how the meaning of equality has evolved and why it continues to challenge and inspire. What makes this endeavour all the more challenging is that equality is not a single, universal idea; it shifts depending on context, culture, and perspective.

These debates suggests that the term 'equality' is perhaps not entirely accurate and should instead be framed as 'equalities' to reflect the diverse perspectives that exist. Indeed, McIntyre J, speaking for the Supreme Court of Canada in *Andrews v Law Society of British Columbia*,[3] remarked that equality 'lacks precise definition'.[4] This stems from its inherently abstract nature, compounded by the abstract words used to define it, as well as its somewhat exalted status,[5] in terms of being widely aspired to but difficult to attain. These factors leave equality open to interpretation, as the concepts used to describe it are often incomplete and heavily influenced by the conceptualiser's view of society and what it should be.[6]

Inspired by Vickers, who argued that different analyses of equality may be suited to different protected grounds,[7] and Fraser, who suggested that 'class inequality is best understood in terms of redistribution, and sexual orientation inequality best

[1] Luyando Martha Katiyatiya and Nombulelo Lubisi, 'Part B: The Role of Substantive Equality in Shaping Transformative Social Protection in South Africa into the Digital Platform Work' (2021) 25 *Journal of Poverty* 23.

[2] Peter Westen, 'The Empty Idea of Equality' (1982) 95 *Harvard Law Review* 537.

[3] *Andrews v The Law Society of British Columbia* [1989] 1 SCR 143, 143 (Supreme Court of Canada).

[4] ibid 164.

[5] *Law v Canada (Minister of Employment and Immigration)* (1999) 1 Supreme Court Rep 497 [507].

[6] Beverley M McLachlin, 'Equality, the Most Difficult Right' (2001) 14 *The Supreme Court Law Review: Osgoode's Annual Constitutional Cases Conference* 17, 20.

[7] Lucy Vickers, 'Promoting Equality or Fostering Resentment? The Public Sector Equality Duty and Religion and Belief' (2011) 31 *Legal Studies* 135, 152.

understood in terms of recognition',[8] I realised that the first step in making sense of equality is to identify which concepts are relevant to the groups that are the subject of inquiry. There are numerous concepts of equality to choose from, which make this process rather daunting.

Rather helpfully, Hepple identified seven meanings of equality: respect for equal worth, dignity and identity as a fundamental human right; eliminating status discrimination and disadvantage; consistent treatment or formal equality; substantive equality of opportunity; equality of capabilities; equality of outcomes; and fairness.[9] McColgan similarly outlined schools of thought on equality, including anti-discrimination; substantive and formal; luck egalitarianism; dignity; social inclusion; and a challenge to oppression.[10] Fredman, in turn, proposed four central principles of equality: breaking the cycle of disadvantage; promoting respect for equal dignity and worth; affirming community identities; and facilitating full participation in society.[11] These frameworks serve as a good starting point for this exercise. Once identified, it should be possible to establish a direct link between relevant concepts and the equality laws that echo them, and to enable an assessment of the law's effectiveness in protecting specific groups.

The second step was inspired by Westen, who explains that equality is sometimes used as a form of shorthand to refer to certain precepts *about* equality, normative axioms whose truth is said to be inherent in or follow from the concept of equality.[12] This contrasts with concepts *of* equality, which effectively particularise these precepts. Therefore, a categorisation exercise of the various concepts of equality is a logical starting point for making sense of the broader debates. What then, are these precepts? Formal, substantive and transformative equality are widely discussed in the literature, and given their distinct aims and standards of measurement, it is possible to categorise various concepts under these precepts. I have therefore adopted them as the precepts of equality for present purposes. Others have done the same, and they have also been referred to as models.[13]

White and others explain that formal equality is needed to have equal status in society, substantive equality is needed to proactively redistribute power and resources, and transformative equality is needed to transform opportunities, institutions and systems so that they are no longer grounded in historical paradigms of power.[14] For instance, if lawmakers promote a formal equality approach, the law will apply equally to all, but ignore the context of inequalities, thus compounding

[8] Nancy Fraser, 'From Redistribution to Recognition? Dilemmas of Justice in a "post-Socialist" Age' in Jeffrey C Alexander and Steven Seidman (eds), *The New Social Theory Reader*, 2nd edn (Routledge, 2008) 68.

[9] Bob Hepple, *Equality: The Legal Framework*, 2nd edn (Hart Publishing, 2014) 18.

[10] Aileen McColgan, *Human Rights Law in Perspective: Discrimination, Equality and the Law* (Bloomsbury, 2014).

[11] Sandra Fredman, 'The Future of Equality in Britain' (Equal Opportunities Commission, 2002) 11–16.

[12] Peter Westen, *Speaking of Equality: An Analysis of the Rhetorical Force of Equality in Moral and Legal Discourse* (Princeton University Press, 1990) 181.

[13] Robyn White and others, 'Court Accommodations for Persons with Severe Communication Disabilities: A Legal Scoping Review.' (2021) 27 *Psychology, Public Policy, and Law* 399.

[14] ibid 399.

the inequalities they seek to eradicate. If they adopt a substantive equality approach instead, they focus on removing or reducing disadvantage for individuals or groups. Perhaps least likely to be adopted is the transformative approach, which seeks to change society's attitudes and implement radical reforms to eliminate inequality. Undertaking such a particularisation process will enable scholars and policymakers to identify which analyses of equality are suited to particular groups, and determine what reforms are needed to achieve equality for these groups.

The next step in this chapter is to look at formal, substantive and transformative equality in detail, and consider the relevant concepts of equality I consider to be associated with each of those precepts.

I. Formal Equality

Formal equality was the dominant theoretical model of equality from the end of the Second World War until the late 1960s[15] and is still considered one of the most prevalent models today.[16] This precept tends to manifest itself in most anti-discrimination law but has been criticised for its potential to justify discriminatory practice.[17] This doctrine has a 'bad rap' and is often 'dismissed as empty, formal and conservative'[18] and 'reductionist'.[19]

To determine if formal equality's imperative is met, a statute's words are examined to see who it covers, and then the law is administered equally to everyone. This method ensures that law is applied consistently and aims to eliminate irrational or arbitrary decision-making. Bartolo provides a good example to illustrate this point:

> In the simplest terms, a formal equality approach means that [social media] platforms prohibit attacks on individuals or groups based on identity factors such as race. However, 'race' is treated as a singular, undifferentiated category: an attack on white people would be treated in the same way as an attack on Black people, for example.[20]

In practice, formal equality disregards people's social context, treating classifications such as gender, race, disability, or other similar status, as irrelevant to the question of

[15] Hepple (n 9) 21.

[16] Equal Rights Trust, 'The Ideas of Equality and Non-Discrimination, Formal and Substantive Equality' (2007), www.equalrightstrust.org/ertdocumentbank/The%20Ideas%20of%20Equality%20and%20Non-discrimination,%20Formal%20and%20Substantive%20Equality.pdf.

[17] Franziska Felder, Laura Davy and Rosemary Kayess (eds), *Disability Law and Human Rights: Theory and Policy* (Springer International Publishing, 2022).

[18] Charles-Maxime Panaccio, '*Apologia* for a General Doctrine of Substantive Equality and Discrimination' (2020) 11 *Jurisprudence* 213, 213.

[19] Felder, Davy and Kayess (n 17) 43.

[20] Louisa Bartolo, '"Eyes Wide Open to the Context of Content": Reimagining the Hate Speech Policies of Social Media Platforms through a Substantive Equality Lens' (2021) 29 *Renewal: A Journal of Social Democracy* 39, 40.

equality.[21] Rather, the focus is on the process of applying and enforcing the law and determining whether everyone covered by the law is treated in the same manner.[22]

Overall, Liisberg argues that while formal equality is relatively straightforward and easier to implement, it fails to address structural disadvantage. As a result, it does not provide a foundation for prohibiting discrimination or enabling positive action.[23] Crucially, it fails to distinguish between treating people equally badly and treating them equally well.[24] Most importantly, formal equality offers an overly simplistic basis for integrated and comprehensive non-discrimination laws and measures, falling short of addressing the richness and complexity of modern life and modern social relations.[25] As a result, it is widely recognised that the formal approach has failed to eliminate entrenched structural, social and economic inequality, highlighting the need for a different approach to tackle the roots of inequality.[26]

Having provided an overview of what formal equality is and how it generally works, I now turn to relevant concepts of equality that fit within this precept, namely equal treatment and equality of opportunity.

A. Equal Treatment

At the heart of formal equality lies the principle of equal treatment, the idea that like cases should be treated alike, focusing on consistent treatment of individuals rather than on achieving any particular outcome.[27] This approach originates from Aristotle, who argued that 'things [and persons] that are alike should be treated alike, while things that are unalike should be treated as unalike in proportion to their unlikeness'.[28]

These are two issues with this approach. First of all, there is no clear criteria for determining in what respect two persons are alike or the basis for comparison.[29] This limitation means that equal treatment cannot address the 'dilemma of difference' as it fails to consider or embrace human difference.[30] Indeed, Holmes argues that no two persons, not even identical twins, are qualitatively alike, thus meaning differences will always exist.[31] This approach also assumes that individuals who are

[21] Sandra Fredman, 'Challenging the Frontiers of Gender Equality: Women at Work' in Rebecca J Cook (ed), *Frontiers of Gender Equality* (University of Pennsylvania Press, 2023).

[22] Donna Greschner, 'Does Law Advance the Cause of Equality' [2001] *Queen's Law Journal* 299, 303.

[23] Maria Ventegodt Liisberg, *Disability and Employment: A Contemporary Disability Human Rights Approach Applied to Danish, Swedish and EU Law and Policy* (Intersentia, 2011) 23.

[24] Fredman (n 21) 41.

[25] Equal Rights Trust (n 16).

[26] Evadne Grant, 'Dignity and Equality' (2007) 7 *Human Rights Law Review* 299, 299.

[27] Vickers (n 7) 147.

[28] Dagmar Schiek, Lisa Waddington and Mark Bell, *Cases, Materials and Text on National, Supranational and International Non-Discrimination Law* (Hart Publishing, 2007) 27.

[29] Nicholas Bamforth, Maleiha Malik and Colm O'Cinneide, *Discrimination Law: Theory and Context, Text and Materials* (Sweet & Maxwell 2008) 178.

[30] Felder, Davy and Kayess (n 17) 39.

[31] Elisa Holmes, 'Anti-Discrimination Rights Without Equality' (2005) 68 *The Modern Law Review* 175, 179.

'different' must either disassociate from their difference or accept it,[32] disregarding the complexities of one's identity. For example, to lodge a formal discrimination complaint, individuals must isolate a single facet of their identity, often at the expense of others.[33] As a result, those who are most 'alike' will reflect the 'benchmark man' or 'dominant white male',[34] typically a white, heterosexual and able-bodied man,[35] reinforcing a powerful pressure toward conformity and assimilation.[36]

Secondly, equal treatment fails to recognise that it is only in some contexts that those characteristics are irrelevant and detrimental, and instead holds out as universal and neutral the characteristics of the dominant group,[37] and fails to address deeper entrenched patterns of social disadvantage.[38] The ongoing effects of past discrimination mean that the opportunities and life course of many continue to be affected by their race, ethnicity or gender.[39] Bourn and Whitmore sum this up well: '[equal treatment's] neutral, symmetrical application of the law ignores the structural and social conditions which form each individual'.[40] What is most frustrating about equal treatment is the law's preoccupation with how people are treated as opposed to the substantive situation they end up in. There is no point having more equal treatment in the world, or requiring people always to treat people equally, if people nevertheless do not end up equally situated.[41]

B. Equality of Opportunity

Equality of opportunity differs from the traditional equal treatment. While equal treatment focuses on the consistent application of rules, equality of opportunity is concerned with fair access to positions of advantage. Roemer identifies two strands of opportunity-based equality: first, society must 'level the playing field' so that everyone can compete fairly; second, only relevant attributes should be used to assess candidates.[42] Flew elaborates that, while such opportunities will not guarantee equal outcomes, they achieve equality by enabling fair and open competition for scarce opportunities.[43] This involves treating all competitors equally without excluding anyone on irrelevant grounds, with the outcome ultimately determined

[32] Liisberg (n 23) 24.

[33] Margaret Thornton, 'Domesticating Disability Discrimination' (1997) 2 *International Journal of Discrimination and the Law* 183, 184.

[34] Fredman (n 21) 40.

[35] Thornton (n 33) 196.

[36] Iris Marion Young, 'Status Inequality and Social Groups' (2002) 2 *Issues in Legal Scholarship* [i], 9.

[37] Sandra Fredman, 'Providing Equality: Substantive Equality and the Positive Duty to Provide' (2005) 21 *South African Journal on Human Rights* 163, 164.

[38] ibid 163.

[39] ibid 165.

[40] Colin Bourn and John Whitmore, *Anti-Discrimination Law in Britain* (Sweet & Maxwell, 1996) paras 1–13.

[41] Holmes (n 31) 179.

[42] John E Roemer, *Equality of Opportunity* (Harvard University Press, 1998) 1.

[43] Anthony Flew, 'Four Kinds of Equality' [1982] *Reason Papers* 17, 22.

by chance or merit. In short, unequal probabilities of success do not necessarily indicate unequal opportunities.[44]

Flew's metaphor of a race for scarce opportunities, where the organisers treat all competitors equally and no one is excluded on irrelevant grounds, offers a helpful lens through which to view equality of opportunity. Fairness lies not in ensuring that every competitor is equally likely to win, but in ensuring that no one is prevented from competing due to characteristics unrelated to the task at hand. As such, this conception aligns equality of opportunity with a meritocratic ideal. Essentially, the merit argument can be represented in the form S merits X in virtue of M, where S is a person, X a mode of treatment or an outcome, and M some feature possessed by S.[45]

McCrudden provides two illustrative examples:

(1) We might say that John (S) merits the award of the sports prize (X) in virtue of having run faster than anyone else competing in the race (M).

(2) Mary (S) merits admission to law school (X) in virtue of her qualities of determination, clarity of thought, and ability to work hard (M), which we think are likely to make her a good lawyer in the future.

What is involved, in other words, is selection of a person for the purposes of distribution of a benefit to that person.[46]

This merit-based conception of equality of opportunity is appealing for its apparent neutrality. It promises a fair and open competition in which individuals succeed based on their abilities and efforts, not irrelevant or discriminatory factors. However, this model assumes that all individuals begin the race from comparable starting points, and that the criteria used to assess merit are themselves impartial. These assumptions are rarely borne out in practice. Structural inequalities, whether social, economic, or historical, often shape both the resources individuals can access and the attributes deemed meritorious. As such, the meritocratic ideal may legitimise unequal outcomes without adequately accounting for the unequal conditions under which merit is produced.

To elaborate on this point, Dworkin argues that equality lies not in the success individuals achieve, but in the value of the resources that they are provided to pursue that success.[47] Sreenivasan echoes this, adding that 'when someone has refused an advantage, their refusal should not count against the justice of its distribution'.[48] What should then be done if the individuals do not have equal value in the resources they have been provided? Fredman suggests that positive measures are needed to ensure all persons share a genuinely equal chance of satisfying the criteria for access to a particular social good.[49] This demands resources for

[44] ibid.

[45] Christopher McCrudden, 'Merit Principles' (1998) 18 *Oxford Journal of Legal Studies* 543, 547.

[46] ibid.

[47] Ronald Dworkin, *Sovereign Virtue: The Theory and Practice of Equality* (Harvard University Press, 2000) back cover.

[48] Gopal Sreenivasan, 'Equality, Opportunity, Ambiguity' (2014) 13 *Politics, Philosophy & Economics* 82, 83.

[49] Fredman (n 37) 167.

education and training, accessibility measures and alternative facilities to effect changes in underlying discriminatory structures and to facilitate effective freedom of choice.[50] This approach muddies the waters somewhat, as what Fredman proposes appears to be substantive in nature, and so equality of opportunity begins to straddle the line between formal and substantive equality.

These insights make clear that achieving equality of opportunity cannot be reduced to formal procedures alone. As Fredman argues, the kinds of positive measures required to create genuine opportunities, that is, education, training, and structural adjustments, begin to move the concept away from its formal roots. This raises an important distinction between equality of opportunity and equality of results. I argue that the former fits within the precept of formal equality, whereas the latter is substantive.

Achieving genuine equality of opportunity requires positive measures to ensure equal access to social goods and address discriminatory structures. Fredman argues that such measures are needed to provide everyone with an equal chance to access resources such as education, training, accessibility provisions and alternative facilities. The former is formal in nature, emphasising equal access to the process, while the latter is substantive, addressing disadvantages experienced by competitors due to specific characteristics.[51]

II. Substantive Equality

The shortcomings of the formal equality precept have led to a search for more substantive concepts of equality, which focus on outcomes and opportunity rather than equal treatment.[52] The main difference is that formal equality implies that all rules apply equally to everyone, while substantive equality examines what the rules should be and analyses their impact on outcomes.[53] In addition, substantive equality addresses the 'dilemma of difference', embracing human diversity.[54] However, Marko warns that formal and substantive should not be seen as opposing concepts but rather as complementary, coexisting within legal frameworks to address different layers of equality.[55]

It is important to bear in mind that substantive equality cannot be defined in terms of a single principle.[56] Instead, it should be seen as a 'catalyst', driving the transformation of socio-political consciousness.[57] To that end, Vickers puts forward

[50] ibid 167.

[51] Fredman (n 37) 167.

[52] Vickers (n 7) 147.

[53] Prabhav Pandey, 'Analysis of the Australian Federal and Victorian Anti-Discrimination Legislation in Achieving the Public Policy Goal of Substantive Equality' (2022) 7 *NUJS Journal of Regulatory Studies* 1.

[54] Yeni Rosdianti, 'Vindicating Substantive Equality in the Right to Work of Persons with Disabilities in Indonesia' (Doctoral Dissertation, National University of Ireland Galway, 2019).

[55] Joseph Marko, 'Against Discrimination' in Joseph Marko and Sergiu Constantin (eds), *Human and Minority Rights Protection by Multiple Diversity Governance*, 1st edn (Routledge, 2019).

[56] Margaret Thornton, 'Equality and Anti-Discrimination Legislation: An Uneasy Relationship' (2021) 37 *Law in Context* 12.

[57] Sawinder Singh, 'Conceptualising "Black Lives Matter": Time to Consider Substantive Equality as a Fundamental Constitutional Guarantee' (2021) 16 *Amity Law Review* 70.

three models of the substantive concept of equality: the link between equality and individual dignity and identity; focusing on disadvantage and distribution; and as a means of addressing social exclusion and promoting participation.[58] Fredman, in turn, outlines four specific aims of substantive equality as follows: to break the cycle of disadvantage[59] associated with out-groups;[60] to promote respect for the equal dignity and worth of all to redress stigma, stereotyping, humiliation and violence due to membership of an out-group; to positively affirm and celebrate identity within community; and to facilitate full participation in society.[61] Albertyn and Goldblatt also believe that disadvantage and difference are core characteristics of substantive equality.[62] These frameworks provide a comprehensive vision of how substantive equality can work in practice.

Generally, substantive equality goes beyond formal equality by requiring the state to take action to address systemic inequalities[63] and promote equality[64] and actively remove obstacles. This involves examining how resources, opportunities, and choices are distributed, which Sinha and others refer to as 'structural transformation'.[65] As laws can significantly impact this distribution, assessing whether a law promotes or impedes substantive equality requires considering people's economic, social, and political circumstances, and examining the distribution of resources.[66] Therefore, evaluating people's circumstances independently of the law itself is essential for such an assessment.

This means substantive equality involves an element of redistribution. This raises important questions about when and to what extent redistribution is justified, issues that have been central to political philosophers such as Rawls, Sen, Dworkin and Cohen.[67] In particular, it is argued that equality of outcome is inherently linked to the redistributive justice model and the achievement of a fairer distribution of benefits.[68] Positive measures can include resource allocation, directly redistributing benefits to address structural disadvantage.[69] Schiek, Waddington and Bell argue that the aim of substantive equality originates not from a theory of law but from a theory of justice, which explains the association

[58] Vickers (n 7) 147.

[59] A disadvantage is a condition or situation that causes problems, especially one that causes something or someone to be less successful than other things or people. (Cambridge Dictionary, 'Disadvantage' [26 March 2025], https://dictionary.cambridge.org/dictionary/english/disadvantage).

[60] Aileen McColgan, *Discrimination Law: Text, Cases and Materials* (Hart Publishing, 2005) 1.

[61] Sandra Fredman, *Discrimination Law*, 1st edn (Oxford University Press, 2002) 167.

[62] Cathi Albertyn and Beth Goldblatt, 'Facing the Challenge of Transformation: Difficulties in the Development of an Indigenous Jurisprudence of Equality' (1998) 14 *South African Journal on Human Rights* 248, 257.

[63] Savitri WE Goonesekere, 'The Indivisibility of Rights and Substantive Equality for Women' in Niamh Reilly (ed), *International Human Rights of Women* (Springer Singapore, 2019).

[64] McColgan (n 60) 22.

[65] Vandna Sinha and others, 'Substantive Equality and Jordan's Principle: Challenges and Complexities' (2021) 35 *Journal of Law and Social Policy* 21.

[66] Greschner (n 22) 303–04.

[67] Bob Hepple, 'The Aims of Equality Law' (2008) 61 *Current Legal Problems* 1, 14.

[68] Equal Rights Trust (n 16).

[69] Judith Fudge, 'Substantive Equality, the Supreme Court of Canada, and the Limits to Redistribution 23: 235.' [2007] *South African Journal on Human Rights* 235.

with distributive justice. However, Fudge highlights a limitation: the redistributive potential of equality rights may remain small[70] due to the reliance on the individual enforcement model to challenge infringements. Conversely, Fredman suggests that implementing substantive equality measures often protects states from having to justify redistributive policies.[71] For instance, states may commit to achieving substantive equality outcomes by providing welfare support for disadvantaged groups. This not only redistributes resources but also signals a political commitment to fulfilling positive duties of provision.[72]

We will now consider some of the relevant analyses of equality that can be categorised as part of the substantive precept.

A. Respect for Equal Worth and Dignity

Human dignity and worth are interesting concepts often associated with substantive equality. They are not earned through an individual's role, achievements, or status but are instead fundamental to being human. As such, they challenge any system that ranks individuals based on such factors and emphasise the equal value of every person.[73] Fredman and Vickers agree that dignity is inherent in the humanity of all people and that no one can be excluded from its reach.[74] Dworkin similarly argues that all people share a right to equal concern and respect, and upholding their equality is an objective good.[75] Respecting human dignity, therefore, means treating everyone with respect due to our common humanity. It also provides redress for stigma, stereotyping, prejudice, and violence.[76]

In terms of worth, Dworkin's principle of 'intrinsic value' reflects that each human life has objective value.[77] Failing to treat a particular group equally reflects a denial of their equal value. In practical terms, when one considers respect for equal worth, it becomes clear that unequal treatment of any group signals their devaluation. Respecting the dignity of the individual also means acknowledging and valuing differences arising from gender, sexuality, disability, or cultural experiences of religion or belief.

Respect for the worth and dignity of each individual plays a central role in modern human rights discussions[78] and serves as a foundation for equality rights.[79] It is expressed in several international treaties, including the Universal Declaration

[70] ibid 244.
[71] Fredman, *Discrimination Law* (n 61) abstract.
[72] ibid 164.
[73] Peter Berger, 'On the Obsolescence of the Concept of Honor' (1970) 11 *European Journal of Sociology* 339.
[74] Sandra Fredman, 'Equality: A New Generation?' (2001) 30 *Industrial Law Journal* 145, 155.
[75] Ronald Dworkin, *Taking Rights Seriously* (Duckworth Press, 1977); Ronald Dworkin, *A Matter of Principle* (Harvard University Press, 1985).
[76] Fredman (n 21).
[77] Hepple (n 67) 8.
[78] Katiyatiya and Lubisi (n 1).
[79] Fredman (n 74) 155.

of Human Rights ('Human Rights Declaration')[80] and the case law of the European Convention on Human Rights ('Human Rights Convention'). For example, Article 1 of the Declaration proclaims that 'all human beings are born free and equal in dignity and rights'. Clearly, the equality and non-discrimination agenda is built on the principle of dignity.[81]

The general consensus is that a focus on dignity does not take the formal equality approach, as it emphasises individual autonomy and dignity over equal treatment.[82] Vickers elaborates that levelling down protections to create parity, such as when aiming for equality of opportunity, may reduce the overall dignity of the groups being compared.[83] Instead, the focus should be on increasing autonomy and dignity enforcing parity of treatment. This approach better accommodates difference and respects individual identities. Interestingly, Iacobucci J ruled in *Law v Canada* that dignity 'does not relate to the status or position of an individual in society *per se*, but rather concerns the manner in which a person legitimately feels when confronted with a particular law',[84] thus firmly embracing a subjective approach to the concept,[85] an approach supported by Reaume, who states that some substantive interest or value must underpin a claim if it is to have any critical bite at all.[86]

Equality as dignity does have a number of shortcomings.[87] These include its conceptual vagueness, its lack of legal precision, and the risk that it could entrench group identities. Terms such as the 'dignity and the equal moral worth of humanity' are imprecise and determining their legal or practical content remains problematic.[88] Greschner argues that the concept of dignity is too vague, general, malleable and emotive to be the core interest protected by equality rights, which should focus on individual interests in belonging to important communities.[89] Moreau concurs that the conception of dignity does not have sufficient content to explain the precise nature of the wrongs done to individuals who are not treated with equal concern and respect.[90]

Vickers explains that the notion of dignity does not assist in determining whether non-discrimination rules need to be introduced, or whether public authorities need to be given interventionist duties.[91] Hepple concurs, stating that 'while dignity is a background value for all human rights, it is too broad and ambiguous to be the basis of equality law'.[92]

[80] Universal Declaration of Human Rights 1948 (A/183/217).
[81] Equal Rights Trust (n 16).
[82] Vickers (n 7) 155.
[83] ibid.
[84] *Law v Canada (Minister of Employment and Immigration)* (n 5) [53].
[85] McColgan (n 60) 25.
[86] Denise G Reaume, 'Discrimination and Dignity' (2003) 63 *Louisiana Law Review* 645, 647.
[87] Vickers (n 7) 149.
[88] ibid 149–50.
[89] Greschner (n 22) 299.
[90] Sophia R Moreau, 'The Wrongs of Unequal Treatment' (2004) 54 *University of Toronto Law Journal* 291, 296.
[91] Vickers (n 7) 150.
[92] Hepple (n 67) 12.

In addition to its conceptual ambiguity and legal imprecision, a dignity-based approach can lead to the reifying of differences between groups. Grabham warns that continued reliance upon concepts such as 'human dignity' and 'individual dignity' can serve to reinforce oppressive norms.[93] This can lead to pressure on individuals to conform to a given group culture or identity, in order to experience the gains of recognition, and the resulting conformity by groups seeking recognition can reduce intra-group discussion and development.

B. Eliminating Status Discrimination and Disadvantage

In contrast to formal equality, substantive equality calls on the state to take proactive measures to promote equality.[94] Looking back at the conception of formal equality of opportunity, it becomes clear that there is a shift towards substantive measures, such as removing obstacles like word-of-mouth recruitment, age limits, or unjustifiable testing, steps that are clearly substantive in nature. However, Fredman acknowledges that these measures alone do not guarantee that disadvantaged individuals can take full advantage of the opportunities available. For example, those lacking qualifications due to past discrimination may still find themselves unable to meet job-related criteria.[95]

Substantive equality also goes beyond the narrow focus of formal equality, addressing the actual distribution of resources, opportunities, and choices within a society. It involves what Bakan calls social equality, in which legislators enact laws to address inequalities in social goods such as income, choices, recognition, and status. By accommodating human diversity and implementing positive measures,[96] substantive equality seeks to challenge the structural and systemic barriers that perpetuate disadvantage. Each new law reshapes these distributions, and an assessment of whether a law promotes or hinders substantive equality requires careful consideration of people's economic, social, and political circumstances, alongside the existing distribution of resources, to understand its impact.[97]

Despite the strengths of eliminating status discrimination and disadvantage, its practical delivery remains uneven. It relies on the dominant culture's standard of measure, which can uphold the status quo. To tackle status discrimination effectively, it is necessary to examine people's circumstances independently of the law itself.[98] Even policies that appear non-discriminatory on their face can inadvertently reinforce existing disparities.[99] When things go wrong, individual

[93] Emily Grabham, 'Law v Canada: New Directions for Equality Under the Canadian Charter?' (2002) 22 *Oxford Journal of Legal Studies* 641, 655.

[94] McColgan (n 60) 22.

[95] Fredman (n 61) 167.

[96] Rosdianti (n 54).

[97] Greschner (n 22) 303–4.

[98] Liisberg (n 23) 304.

[99] Judy McGregor and Sharyn Graham Davies, 'Achieving Pay Equity: Strategic Mobilization for Substantive Equality in Aotearoa New Zealand' (2019) 26 *Gender, Work & Organization* 619.

enforcement of rights through the courts becomes necessary, often placing a heavy burden on those already disadvantaged. O'Cinneide describes this model as akin to sending a fire engine to fight a fire rather than preventing that fire in the first place:[100] reactive rather than proactive and negative rather than positive.[101]

C. Equality of Outcome and Results

Equality of outcome (or results) represents the most interventionist form of equality, grounded in the view that fairness requires not just access or opportunity, but actual parity in outcomes between groups. It goes beyond formal equality and demands not only equal outcomes[102] but also the addressing of stigma, stereotyping, and structural barriers.[103] It considers whether equal treatment has adversely affected individuals due to their individual characteristics. For example, systems of political representation should deliver equal outcomes between genders and ethnicities. However, the equal right to vote and stand for election does not necessarily result in parity between sexes or ethnicities. To achieve equality of outcome, additional measures such as quotas, may be necessary.[104] Equality of outcome is more relevant when comparing groups rather than individuals,[105] and policies like reverse discrimination, positive discrimination, and positive action represent this concept.[106] Sinha and others emphasise that equitable outcomes are the primary indicator of substantive equality.[107]

Equality of opportunity and results are closely linked – and must be considered simultaneously[108] – with the former representing the primary objective and equality of outcome serving as the test for determining whether the objective has been met. When outcomes differ, it is often because opportunities were unequal.[109] Equality of opportunity focuses on procedures and individuals, while equality of outcome focuses on groups and the results achieved.[110] These procedures must themselves be fair, accessible, and free from systemic barriers.[111] These two concepts are therefore not necessarily opposing but complementary.

[100] Colm O'Cinneide, 'Beyond the Limits of Equal Treatment: The Use of Positive Duties in Equality Law' (Mainstreaming Equality: Models for a Statutory Duty, Equality Authority, Dublin, Ireland, 27 February 2003) 21.

[101] Dominique Allen, 'Rethinking the Australian Model of Promoting Gender Equality' in Katharine G Young and Kim Rubenstein (eds), *The Public Law of Gender: From the Local to the Global* (Cambridge University Press, 2016) 405.

[102] Anne Phillips, 'Defending Equality of Outcome' [2004] *Journal of Political Philosophy* 1, 16.

[103] Fredman (n 21).

[104] Phillips (n 102) 11.

[105] ibid 24.

[106] Equal Rights Trust (n 16).

[107] Sinha and others (n 65).

[108] Fredman (n 21).

[109] Phillips (n 102) 10.

[110] E Andreevska and E Aziri, 'Principle of Equality in International Law: The Right to Equality' (2009) 2 *Lex ET Scientia International Journal* 228, 236.

[111] Sinha and others (n 65).

To illustrate the difference between equality of opportunity and equality of results, consider that no person has a right to a high-paying job or to a university place; instead, everyone has a right to compete, on the basis of merit, for jobs and university admission. While equal opportunity is recognised as a human right, equality of results is not.[112] Andreevska and Aziri argue that the effective enforcement of anti-discrimination can generate equality of opportunity for all members of society. However, enforcement of such laws will not produce equality of results. Sinha and others support the idea that processes and outcomes must be intertwined to address systemic inequalities.[113] To move towards equality of results, governments would need to rely on redistributive measures such as taxation and increased spending on health, education, and welfare,[114] a point supported by Fredman.[115]

Equality of results is not without its criticisms, however. McColgan suggests that it merely serves a diagnostic purpose, in that it highlights the existence of obstacles rather than suggests an outcome, and is therefore an insufficient basis of equality law.[116] Essentially, equality of results equalises where people end up rather than where or how they begin (equality of opportunity), and Phillips argues that this approach lacks sophistication as it immediately begs the question of what it is we are seeking to equalise. Is the aim to equalise income, happiness or welfare, or all three?[117] Another perceived danger of this approach is that it places too little emphasis on the importance of accommodating diversity by adapting existing structures. In this regard some argue that focusing on certain predefined social groups may misdirect attention away from deeper, more arbitrary sources of disadvantage.[118]

Nonetheless, equality of outcome is a powerful tool for exposing entrenched inequalities and reframing the goals of equality law beyond individual treatment.

III. Transformative Equality

Transformative equality is a yet largely undeveloped precept of equality,[119] as much of the focus remains on the distinction between formal and substantive equality. It aims to dismantle systemic inequalities and eradicate poverty and disadvantage by ensuring 'equality of capabilities',[120] removing barriers, redistributing resources, and developing opportunities that enable people to realise their full potential

[112] Andreevska and Aziri (n 110) 236.
[113] Sinha and others (n 65).
[114] Andreevska and Aziri (n 110).
[115] Fredman (n 21).
[116] Aileen McColgan, 'Cracking the Comparator Problem: Discrimination, "Equal" Treatment and the Role of Comparisons' [2006] *European Human Rights Law Review* 650, 671.
[117] Phillips (n 102) 2.
[118] Equal Rights Trust (n 16).
[119] Cochav Elkayam-Levy, 'Re-Imagining the Rules - The Global Transition to Transformative Equality and the Narratives of Feminist Religious Movements' (2021), https://papers.ssrn.com/sol3/papers.cfm?abstract_id=3757963.
[120] Sandra Fredman, 'Substantive Equality Revisited' (2016) 14 *International Journal of Constitutional Law* 712, 730

within positive social relationships.[121] O'Cinneide emphasises that transformative equality involves advancing equality claims by targeting entrenched structural inequalities and addressing their root causes by examining socio-economic conditions, identifying systemic disadvantages, and implementing proactive measures through public bodies and institutional reforms.[122] It is also referred to as the 'proactive model', the 'multidimensional disadvantage model', the 'diversity equality model',[123] and 'inclusive equality'.[124] It is clear that the literature has tended to focus on what it is, but is least explicit about how to achieve it. While Loveday suggests that a transformative analysis should pay attention to structural injustice at institutional, political, economic, and societal levels,[125] Cusack and Pusey underline the importance of challenging harmful norms, prejudices, and stereotypes to shift social attitudes,[126] and Farid and others suggest that institutions themselves need to be restructured and the harmful norms and beliefs embedded in the institutions need to be addressed,[127] they do not specify exactly this could be done.

How then, do we achieve transformative equality? In practical terms, O'Cinneide suggests that this can be achieved by first examining the socio-economic conditions of the individuals and groups concerned, and second, identifying the impact of the impugned provision on social patterns and systemic forms of disadvantage. The grounds of discrimination should be looked at in an intersectional manner in order to ascertain the complex and compounded nature of group disadvantage and privilege.[128] More recently, O'Cinneide suggests that this process will involve policy development, institutional reforms, stakeholder engagement, monitoring and evaluation, capacity building and legislative action.[129]

Another approach is through 'transformative reparations', with McGonigle, Leyh and Fraser expanding the concept of reparations, which has traditionally included financial compensation, rehabilitation, apologies or memorials, to perhaps providing education and job training to victims to improve their socio-economic status, investing in infrastructure and services in marginalised communities, and implementing changes in the law and institutions to prevent further violations.[130]

[121] Cathi Albertyn and Beth Goldblatt, 'Facing the Challenge of Transformation: Difficulties in the Development of an Indigenous Jurisprudence of Equality' (1998) 14 *South African Journal on Human Rights* 248, 249.

[122] Colm O'Cinneide, 'Equality, Rights and the "Stickiness" of the Current Political Moment' in Kalina Arabadjieva and others (eds), *Transformative Ideas – Ensuring a Just Share of Progress for All* (ETUI aisbl, 2023).

[123] ibid 47.

[124] Felder, Davy and Kayess (n 17).

[125] Loveday Hodson, 'Gender and the International Judge: Towards a Transformative Equality Approach' (2022) 35 *Leiden Journal of International Law* 913.

[126] Simone Cusack and Lisa Pusey, 'CEDAW and the Rights to Non-Discrimination and Equality' (2013) 14 *Melbourne Journal of International Law* 54.

[127] Anis Farid and others, 'Negotiating Ideations: The Role of State-Led Identity-Making in the Progress of Women's Rights in Malaysia' (2022) 23 *Australian Journal of Asian Law* 9.

[128] Colm O'Cinneide, 'Fumbling Towards Coherence: The Slow Evolution of Equality and Anti-Discrimination Law in Britain' (2006) 57 *Northern Ireland Legal Quarterly* 57, 262.

[129] O'Cinneide (n 122).

[130] Brianne McGonigle Leyh and Julie Fraser, 'Transformative Reparations: Changing the Game or More of the Same?' (2019) 8 *Cambridge International Law Journal* 39.

Finally, O'Brien suggests that transformative equality can be achieved through including the voices and experiences of individuals in the development of implementation of policies and practices that affect them, community-based approaches, holistic frameworks and participatory governance.[131]

These propositions can be grouped into five themes: understanding and addressing the socio-economic conditions that lead to inequality; undertaking intersectional analysis to explore how overlapping forms of discrimination can compound disadvantage; pursuing structural and institutional reform; embracing transformative reparations; and ensuring participation and inclusion in decision-making processes.

Wider afield, to be effective, transformative equality requires a 'triangular relationship' between internal scrutiny, involvement of interest groups, and an enforcement agency – what Hepple refers to as a 'reflexive regulation approach'.[132] This involves three interlocking mechanisms, with the first being internal scrutiny by the organisation itself to ensure effective self-regulation. The second is the involvement of interest groups (such as managers, employees and service users) who must be informed, consulted and engaged in the process of change. The third is an enforcement agency which should provide the back-up role of assistance, building capabilities and ultimately sanctioning where voluntary methods fail. This reflexive regulation should focus on removing oppressive institutional structures to achieve meaningful social and political participation for particular groups.[133]

The weakness of the transformative approach is the reliance on policymakers to amend existing social structures,[134] which then means that outgroups are at the mercy of politicians, governments and the legislature, who will have their own priorities to work through. Achieving transformative equality would require a seismic shift in society's attitudes, in itself a challenge because any such change would need to be sustained, requiring both a transformational change and a transformational approach.[135] Nonetheless, transformative equality is preferable to substantive equality as it focuses on structures that exclude people from participating in determining their actions, namely decision-making power, the division of labour and culture, or the symbolic meanings attached to people, actions and things, rather than the distributive paradigm prevalent in substantive equality.[136]

We will now explore a selection of theoretical approaches to equality that exemplify the transformative precept.

[131] Nick O'Brien, 'Postliberal Accountability: The Challenge of Disability Human Rights' in *Politics and Administrative Justice: Postliberalism, Street-Level Bureaucracy and the Reawakening of Democratic Citizenship* (Bristol University Press, 2023).

[132] Bob Hepple, 'Enforcing Equality Law: Two Steps Forward and Two Steps Backwards for Reflexive Regulation' (2011) 40 *Industrial Law Journal* 315, 321.

[133] O'Brien (n 131).

[134] Hepple (n 132).

[135] Elkayam-Levy (n 119).

[136] Irene M Young, *Justice and the Politics of Difference* (Princeton University Press, 1990).

A. Social Inclusion

The full inclusion of disabled people in employment depends on broader access to education, housing, transport, healthcare, and daily living support. Collins argues that UK equality law is underpinned by a central organising principle of social inclusion, offering a coherent explanation for why anti-discrimination law prohibits certain forms of harm to excluded groups.[137] At its most basic, for social inclusion to happen minority groups need to be encouraged to participate in civic life to end their marginalisation.[138] This idea situates equality law within a wider policy landscape aimed at addressing social exclusion through government initiatives.[139] However, 'social inclusion' is arguably more conceptually ambiguous than traditional principles like equal treatment or equal opportunity.[140] What does social inclusion set out to do? To make sense of that, we first need to ask: what is exclusion? Without answering that, we cannot begin to understand what inclusion requires; or whether it is working.

As a starting point, social inclusion is the logical antonym of social exclusion.[141] Levitas offers a broader sociological account of social exclusion, distinguishing between three ways it is commonly understood in policy discourse.[142] The first, known as the redistributionist discourse (RED), views exclusion as the result of poverty and lack of material resources. For example, someone may be socially excluded because they cannot afford adequate housing, transport, or food. The second, the social integrationist discourse (SID), defines exclusion in terms of not participating in the labour market, that is, being unemployed or not economically productive. Under this framing, the solution to exclusion is usually seen as getting people 'back to work'. The third, the moral underclass discourse (MUD), takes a more judgemental stance, portraying excluded individuals as responsible for their own situation due to perceived behavioural failings such as laziness, criminality, or a lack of personal responsibility. This discourse is evident in policy approaches that emphasise sanctions, moral reform, or 'cracking down' on the so-called undeserving poor.[143]

Levitas argues that UK social policy has largely been shaped by the second of these, the SID approach, which positions employment as the primary route to inclusion.[144] This narrow focus, she suggests, has also influenced how social inclu-

[137] Hugh Collins, 'Discrimination, Equality and Social Inclusion' (2003) 66 *The Modern Law Review* 16.

[138] Vickers (n 7) 154.

[139] O'Cinneide (n 128) 63.

[140] Hepple (n 67) 21.

[141] Donna Koller, Morgane Le Pouesard and Joanna Anneke Rummens, 'Defining Social Inclusion for Children with Disabilities: A Critical Literature Review' (2018) 32 *Children & Society* 1; Michael A Peters and Tina AC Besley, 'Social Exclusion/Inclusion: Foucault's Analytics of Exclusion, the Political Ecology of Social Inclusion and the Legitimation of Inclusive Education' (2014) 1 *Open Review of Educational Research* 99.

[142] Ruth Levitas, *The Inclusive Society?: Social Exclusion and New Labour*, 2nd edn (Palgrave Macmillan, 2005).

[143] ibid 7–8.

[144] ibid 21–27.

sion is understood within equality law, where access to work or services is often treated as the main indicator of equality. Levitas and others point out that the term social exclusion is often used in different and inconsistent ways, with people making assumptions about what causes exclusion without always examining the underlying social or economic structures that sustain it.[145] To address this, they introduce the Bristol Social Exclusion Matrix (B-SEM), a multidimensional model that takes into account the economic, social, and political conditions that contribute to exclusion over time.[146]

Now that we have examined exclusion, what, then, is meant by inclusion? Under the RED framework, inclusion involves the reduction of poverty and increased access to material resources. In the SID model, as established above, inclusion is understood as re-entry into the labour market. In contrast, MUD frames inclusion as conditional on behavioural change, whereby individuals must alter their conduct in order to be deemed worthy of reintegration. B-SEM takes a broader view, conceptualising inclusion as requiring access to economic resources, essential services, political participation, cultural opportunities and social networks. These perhaps provide us with a practical application of inclusion, but what it means remains elusive.[147]

A number of scholars have attempted to pin down the concept of social inclusion, although definitions vary considerably across contexts. Oxoby argues that inclusion is not only about access to institutions or opportunities, but also about individuals' perception that they can engage meaningfully in society; inclusion, in this view, has both structural and psychological dimensions.[148] Similarly, Alexiadou critiques the way education policy in England has framed inclusion narrowly around employability, noting that such interpretations often overlook structural inequalities and the broader power relations that shape exclusion.[149]

In the context of the European Union, Atkinson identifies a shift from poverty alleviation to a model of inclusion centred on labour market participation and social investment, yet questions remain about how far this model addresses underlying disadvantage.[150] Meanwhile, Cordier and others, in a systematic review of inclusion measures, find that the concept is inconsistently defined and often reduced to observable outcomes such as community participation, with limited attention to subjective experience or structural conditions.[151] Together, these

[145] Ruth Levitas and others, 'The Multidimensional Analysis of Social Exclusion' (University of Bristol, 2007), 28, https://dera.ioe.ac.uk/id/eprint/6853/1/multidimensional.pdf.

[146] ibid 10.

[147] Ana Belén Cano-Hila, 'Understanding Social Inclusion in Contemporary Society: Challenges, Reflections, Limitations, and Proposals' (2022) 10 *Social Inclusion* 1, 1.

[148] Robert Oxoby, 'Understanding Social Inclusion, Social Cohesion, and Social Capital' (2009) 36 *International Journal of Social Economics* 1133.

[149] Nafsika Alexiadou, 'Social Inclusion and Social Exclusion in England: Tensions in Education Policy' (2002) 17 *Journal of Education Policy* 71.

[150] Tony Atkinson, 'Social Inclusion and the European Union' (2002) 40 *Journal of Common Market Studies* 625.

[151] Reinie Cordier and others, 'A Systematic Review Evaluating the Psychometric Properties of Measures of Social Inclusion' (2017) 12 *PLOS ONE* e0179109.

perspectives reinforce the idea that inclusion, as currently framed in policy and practice, may lack the conceptual clarity and transformative ambition required to achieve genuine equality.

It becomes clear that the conceptual limits of social inclusion are increasingly acknowledged. While anti-discrimination law can remove barriers to participation, its transformative potential, to reshape discriminatory norms and structures, is often more aspirational than real.[152] Barnard proposes that the legal framework should instead be rooted in the value of solidarity, which she argues is preferable to inclusion alone, as it imposes both a negative obligation to remove barriers and a positive obligation to take active steps toward integration.[153] This raises the question of whether social inclusion, as currently understood, is capable of delivering the kind of structural change demanded by a transformative conception of equality.

One of the most significant limitations of social inclusion is its tendency to equate inclusion with access. Inclusion becomes a question of whether an individual can enter a space to access a service, attend school, or participate in employment, rather than whether they can participate meaningfully, on an equal footing, within it. This approach risks treating access as the end point of equality, rather than the starting point. It obscures the structural and cultural barriers that remain even when legal or physical entry is granted. Levitas has critiqued this narrow framing, showing how dominant policy discourses define inclusion through labour market participation, without interrogating the deeper inequalities it leaves intact.[154] Oxoby similarly argues that inclusion requires not only access and opportunity, but also the perceived ability to engage meaningfully in society, highlighting its relational and psychological dimensions as well as its structural ones.[155] The result is what has been described elsewhere as the illusion of inclusion,[156] a condition in which individuals may be present within institutions or systems, but on terms that do not enable genuine equality or transformation.

B. Challenging Oppression

Oppression is defined by Young as 'the institutional constraint on self-development',[157] and to be oppressed is to be inhibited from 'developing and exercising one's capacities and expressing one's experience'.[158] Young elaborates:

[152] Vickers (n 7) 154.
[153] Catherine Barnard, 'The Future of Equality Law: Equality and Beyond' in Simon Deakin, Catherine Barnard and Gillian S Morris (ed), *The Future of Labour Law. Liber Amicorum Sir Bob Hepple* (Hart Publishing, 2004) 227.
[154] Levitas (n 142).
[155] Oxoby (n 148).
[156] Maartje De Meulder and Hilde Haualand, 'Sign Language Interpreting Services: A Quick Fix for Inclusion?' (World Association of Sign Language Interpreters Conference, Paris, France, 15 July 2019).
[157] Young (n 136) 37.
[158] ibid.

> Oppression consists in systematic institutional processes which prevent some people from learning and using satisfying and expansive skills in socially recognised settings, or institutional processes which inhibit people's ability to play and communicate with others or to express their feelings and perspectives on social life in contexts where others can listen.[159]

In this way, oppression reflects a broader set of social and institutional constraints than those typically addressed by formal or even substantive models of equality. While formal equality is concerned with equal treatment, and substantive equality with outcomes and disadvantage, the focus here is on the ways in which institutions restrict participation, expression and recognition. It therefore requires a different kind of response, one that engages with social norms, power relations and institutional practices.

Young therefore criticises the individualistic focus of equality law and calls for a justice framework attentive to structural and institutional dynamics, including the distribution of power, cultural representation, and access to decision-making. This approach reframes discrimination as a form of group-based oppression, not merely individual unfairness.[160] There are 'five faces of oppression' – exploitation, marginalisation, powerlessness, cultural imperialism and violence[161] – which are not intended as a complete theory, but rather as a set of diagnostic criteria. As she explains, they are objective conditions that can be assessed through 'observable behaviour, status relationships, distributions, texts and other cultural artifacts'.[162] There have been attempts to apply these five faces to map intersecting forms of oppression within specific institutional or social contexts, with recent applications including Hernández González's climate justice analysis,[163] Dodenhoff's examination of disability hate crime in the UK,[164] and Liao and Carbonell's critique of medical technologies.[165]

Let us briefly explore these five faces of oppression. Exploitation refers to the structural relation between social groups, where the have-nots expend their energies to maintain and augment the power, status, and wealth of the haves. Marginalisation refers to the expulsion of people from useful participation in social life, leading to severe material deprivation and even extermination.[166] Powerlessness refers to a lack of authority, status and sense of self, while cultural

[159] ibid 38.
[160] Bamforth, Malik and O'Cinneide (n 29) 224–25.
[161] Young (n 136) 42.
[162] ibid 64.
[163] Juanita Hernández González, 'Applying the Five Faces of Oppression to Climate Justice: Analysing Discussions of Climate Justice with the Help of Iris Marion Young's Theory of Oppression' (Master's Dissertation, Utrecht University, 2021), https://studenttheses.uu.nl/bitstream/handle/20.500.12932/40655/Thesis%205936381%202_06_2021%20%281%29.pdf?sequence=1&isAllowed=y.
[164] Paul Dodenhoff, 'Five Faces of Oppression - Disability Hate Crime in the UK' (*Disabled World*, 14 May 2014), www.disabled-world.com/disability/discrimination/faces.php.
[165] Shen-yi Liao and Vanessa Carbonell, 'Materialized Oppression in Medical Tools and Technologies' (2023) 23 *The American Journal of Bioethics* 9.
[166] Young, *Justice and the Politics of Difference* (n 136) 48.

imperialism involves the universalisation of a dominant group's experience and culture, and its establishment as the norm, involving 'the paradox of experiencing oneself as invisible at the same time that one is marked out as different'.[167] Finally, violence refers to systematic violence directed at members of a group simply because they are members of a group.[168]

While Young's five faces of oppression have achieved critical acclaim, it is not without its criticisms. Its scale, which allows it to be applied to various social contexts, also risks diluting its analytical precision.[169] For instance, not every form of substantive disadvantage will neatly map onto one of the five faces, and the framework does not always specify how the harms it identifies can be remedied. Indeed, the focus remains primarily descriptive: the five faces help to diagnose oppression but offer limited guidance on how to dismantle the systems that sustain it.[170] As such, the framework may help to expose structural inequality without necessarily generating transformative responses. Additionally, critics have noted that the model tends to treat group identities as relatively stable and is less well equipped to engage with intersectional or shifting forms of marginalisation.[171] These limitations do not undermine the framework's value, but they do suggest the need to locate it within a broader transformative approach to equality, one that moves beyond analysis and towards structural change.

C. To Facilitate Full Participation in Society

Fraser advocates for full participation in society as one of four dimensions to achieve substantive equality,[172] but its significance becomes even more pronounced when situated within a transformative framework. Participation, Fraser argues, should enable those most affected by inequality to shape the decisions that govern their lives. It is especially vital for those whose voices are routinely unheard within traditional governance or legal structures, particularly as both lack of recognition and economic disadvantage can impede full participation in social life, due to lack of confidence or esteem, or lack of resources.[173] Rosdianti similarly observes that participation must actively promote the involvement of affected groups in policymaking processes, and links this to the role of positive duties in equality law.[174]

[167] ibid.
[168] ibid.
[169] Nancy Fraser, *Justice Interruptus: Critical Reflections on the 'Postsocialist' Condition* (Routledge, 1997); Kristie Dotson, 'Conceptualizing Epistemic Oppression' (2014) 28 *Social Epistemology* 115.
[170] Maeve McKeown, 'Structural Injustice' (2021) 16 *Philosophy Compass* e12757.
[171] Kimberlé Williams Crenshaw, 'Race, Reform, and Retrenchment: Transformation and Legitimation in Antidiscrimination Law' (1988) 101 *Harvard Law Review* 1331; Kimberle Crenshaw, 'Mapping the Margins: Intersectionality, Identity Politics, and Violence Against Women of Color' (1991) 43 *Stanford Law Review* 1241.
[172] Fredman (n 120) 727.
[173] ibid.
[174] Rosdianti (n 54).

Participation can be a tool of transformation because it is potentially emancipatory for those involved, enabling individuals to articulate their experiences, needs and concerns.[175] Increased participation in public life, education and employment will follow on from political and social recognition of, and valuing of, individual identity, because it creates the self-confidence in individuals which is necessary for them to flourish and take advantage of the opportunities available. Thus, it is argued, the recognising and valuing of group and individual identity increases social inclusion and leads to greater economic equality.[176]

Katiyatiya and Lubisi reinforce this view by linking participation with multiple systems of integration: political, legal, economic, and social.[177] While they use these systems of integration to analyse social inclusion, the same systems provide a useful frame for understanding participation. There is an important distinction: where inclusion is concerned with ensuring individuals can access and engage in these systems, participation asks whether that engagement enables structurally marginalised groups to influence the design, priorities, and norms of those systems themselves.[178]

It is clear that participation needs to be active if interventions are to avoid being patronising, erroneous or unsuccessful.[179] Decisions need to be made by consulting with a greater range of voices to meet the need of all groups.[180] It is also only meaningful when supported by access to information, education, and deliberative platforms, which many marginalised groups lack.[181] Cornwall calls this 'invited participation', which, while offering seats at the table, often does so without the support necessary to exercise meaningful influence.[182] In addition, consultation is often used as a means of legitimising already made decisions, providing only a 'thin veneer of participation' that may not influence outcomes at all.[183] Gaventas argues that participation can easily become performative if people are not first equipped to recognise their right to speak and to challenge the power structures stacked against them. Without that foundation, even well-meaning participatory spaces risk being taken over by dominant actors, ultimately reinforcing the very inequalities they claim to address.[184] O'Cinneide elaborates on this point, stating that participatory processes assume that everyone who participates has a more or less equal chance of influencing and participating in democratic processes, which is 'out of step with reality'.[185]

[175] McGonigle Leyh and Fraser (n 130) 48.
[176] Vickers (n 7) 154–5.
[177] Katiyatiya and Lubisi (n 1) 34.
[178] ibid.
[179] McColgan (n 60) 29.
[180] Vickers (n 7) 154.
[181] Katiyatiya and Lubisi (n 1).
[182] Andrea Cornwall, 'Unpacking "Participation": Models, Meanings and Practices' (2008) 43 *Community Development Journal* 269, 280–81.
[183] ibid 270.
[184] John Gaventa, 'Finding the Spaces for Change: A Power Analysis' (2006) 37 *IDS Bulletin* 23, 29–30.
[185] O'Cinneide (n 122) 68.

The concepts associated with transformative equality, participation, oppression, and social inclusion, have particular resonance in the context of deaf experience. Chapter five returns to these themes, not to repeat them, but to explore how they are reinterpreted, challenged, or expanded through what I term the Deaf Equality Concepts.

IV. Conclusion

This chapter has exposed us to wide ranging concepts of equality. Following a categorisation exercise of these concepts into precepts or emerging rocks of certainty, we then embarked on an exploration of some of the concepts associated with each precept and attempted to critique them. In order to undertake this challenging task, a precept methodology was utilised, whereby formal, substantive and transformative equality were used as the three main categories of equality, within which concepts of equality were found to be more closely aligned to certain precepts than others.

Therefore, formal equality expects individuals to be treated like for like. Generally speaking, it expects decision-makers to apply laws equally to all without examining in any detail any particular circumstances or the context of the individual, providing a seemingly objective approach in determining whether such an individual has experienced inequality in any given situation. Substantive equality, in contrast to formal equality, requires the state to adopt more positive measures to promote equality, and moves away from the formal focus on equal treatment. It will consider individuals' circumstances independently of the law itself. The precept of transformative equality expects difference and ignores norms against which all others are to be compared. There seems to be a wide consensus among scholars that transformative equality may go some way to dismantle systemic inequalities, as it has been established that it is these that formal and substantive equality do not quite manage to eliminate.

In summary, a useful analogy that best explains the role the three precepts of equality play are of inequality as a disease, and formal, substantive and transformative equality being three different types of treatment. Effectively, formal and substantive measures tend to only treat the symptoms of inequality, whereas transformative equality will treat the disease itself. To eradicate the disease that is inequality altogether must be a preferable solution to merely alleviating or addressing individual acts of inequality, without making inroads in its 'curing'.

As we now proceed to chapter three's exploration of equality law in practice, Hepple provides a word of warning: 'no-one should pretend that all inequality can be remedied by law'.[186] Bearing in mind that the concept of equality has a multiple of philosophical interpretations, underpinned by precepts of equality and fleshed out by various examples, it goes without saying that if the concept of equality itself cannot be pinned down, how is it possible for law-makers to legislate in order to afford individuals equality rights?

[186] Hepple (n 132) 22.

3

The Deaf Legal Illusion

You might think that with the European Convention on Human Rights ('the Human Rights Convention')[1]; the United Nations Convention for the Rights of Persons with Disabilities[2] ('the Disability Convention'); and the Equality Act 2010 (EqA 2010), and all the case law in between, deaf people would be well protected. But 'legal' protection is not the same as 'lived' protection. The law might speak the language of rights and equality, but when deaf people rely on it, the cracks begin to show.

In fact, the law often offers something closer to what De Meulder and Haualand have called the 'illusion of inclusion': symbolic access that hides deeper structural exclusion; interpreters instead of language-concordant services; individual adjustments instead of systemic transformation.[3] This chapter builds on that critique by introducing the concept of the Deaf Legal Illusion, the idea that legal frameworks appear to include deaf people, but do so on terms that are functionally disabling, culturally misaligned, and ultimately ineffective. This illusion is reinforced through legislation that names deaf people as rights-holders, yet rarely centres their actual linguistic, cultural, or community needs. The result is a system in which the law seems to protect, but in practice excludes, through inaccessible procedures, narrow definitions, and impossible burdens of enforcement.

The question this chapter asks is deceptively simple: how far does equality law really go in protecting deaf people? And the answer, as ever, lies not in what the law says, but in what it assumes, and what it ignores. Rather than analysing each legal instrument in turn, this chapter takes a thematic approach, tracing how deaf people are positioned or mispositioned within frameworks that promise inclusion but often deliver something closer to compliance.

Section I begins by setting out the international and domestic instruments under review. Section II unpacks how deaf people are defined under equality law, and the consequences of that definition. Law is never neutral, and the framing of disability carries cultural and political weight. Section III turns to reasonable adjustments (or accommodation) and asks what is considered 'reasonable' and who gets to decide. I argue that reasonableness often hinges on whether adjustments are

[1] Convention for the Protection of Human Rights and Fundamental Freedoms 1950 (4XI1950).

[2] United Nations, Convention on the Rights of Persons with Disabilities A/61/611 (2006), www.un.org/disabilities/documents/convention/convoptprot-e.pdf.

[3] Maartje De Meulder and Hilde Haualand, 'Sign Language Interpreting Services: A Quick Fix for Inclusion?' (World Association of Sign Language Interpreters Conference, Paris, France, 15 July 2019).

one-off or ongoing, and whether human rights risks are involved, a standard that consistently disadvantages deaf claimants. Section IV investigates how the equality and monitoring duties under the Disability Convention and the EqA 2010 operate in practice. Are they tools of transformation, or just tick-box exercises? Finally, the chapter looks at enforcement: what recourse do deaf individuals actually have when they face discrimination? And what happens when deafness intersects with race, gender, sexuality or class, categories the law too often treats as separate?

Throughout, the chapter asks whether equality law offers real protection or is emblematic of the Deaf Legal Illusion.

I. The Legal Instruments under Scrutiny

Equality law in the UK draws on a patchwork of domestic legislation and international rights instruments that, on the surface, appear to offer strong protections for deaf people. Each promises equality in principle. Each falls short in practice. This section briefly introduces each instrument, not to restate their content in full, but to highlight their relevance, and limitations, in the UK context. Together, they reveal a central theme in this chapter: the gap between what the law appears to offer and what it actually delivers. That is the core of the Deaf Legal Illusion.

A. The Human Rights Convention

The Convention is widely regarded as the most effective international instrument for the protection of individual rights and is our first example of formal equality.[4] It contains provisions such as the individual's right to be informed, in a language that they understand, of the reasons for their arrest and charges against them, and to the free assistance of an interpreter if they cannot understand or speak the language used in court. At first glance, the Convention appears to have immense relevance to deaf people, and provides them with a means of enforcing rights such as the right to life and to protect from torture, slavery and forced labour; the right to a fair trial; the right of privacy and to a family life; the right to freedom of thought, conscience, and religion, and to expression; and the right to associate and assemble.

B. The Disability Convention

Meanwhile, the Disability Convention, adopted in 2006, sets out what human rights mean in the context of disabilities. The first human rights treaty of the twenty-first century represents a major step towards realising the right of disabled people to be

[4] Laurence R Helfer, 'Consensus, Coherence and the European Convention' (1993) 26 *Cornell International Law Journal* 133, 133.

treated as full and equal citizens.[5] The provisions of the Disability Convention are of particular relevance to deaf people in that they refer to national sign languages, which is the first time that an international human rights instrument has referred to deaf people as a language group. This recognition is significant because it shifts the framing of deaf people away from a purely medical model of disability toward an acknowledgment of their linguistic and cultural identity.

The provisions of the Disability Convention include a requirement for state parties to the treaty to provide professional sign language interpreters to facilitate accessibility to buildings and other facilities open to the public and in the context of freedom of expression and opinion, accepting and facilitating the use of sign languages, and recognising and promoting the use of sign languages. In terms of education, the Disability Convention stipulates that state parties should facilitate the learning of sign language, promote the linguistic identity of deaf communities and take appropriate measures to employ teachers, including teachers with disabilities, who are qualified in sign language. Finally, the Disability Convention recognises that deaf people are entitled to the recognition and support of their specific cultural and linguistic identities, including sign languages and deaf culture. This is due to the express inclusion of deaf people as sign language users, and in doing so promoting equal worth, dignity and identity. As a result, the Disability Convention is considered potentially transformative.

C. The Equality Act

In the UK, the Disability Discrimination Act 1995 (DDA 1995) was the first anti-discrimination legislation affording disabled people protection. Bamforth, Malik and O'Cinneide suggest that the DDA 1995 broke new ground in its rejection of a symmetrical approach, reminiscent of formal equality, and the imposition of positive accommodation duties upon employers and service providers[6] representative of a substantive approach. Thus, the DDA 1995 was the first piece of anti-discrimination legislation in the UK that promoted a substantive equality of opportunity approach by imposing the duty to make reasonable adjustments on employers, service providers and educational institutions. The DDA 1995 was subsequently amalgamated into the EqA 2010. This retains much of the formal equality approach within its provisions, particularly in relation to what conduct is prohibited (that is, direct discrimination, indirect discrimination, harassment, victimisation and discrimination arising from disability), although its reasonable adjustments remain substantive, and the public sector equality duty potentially transformative.

[5] Equality and Human Rights Commission, 'UN Convention on the Rights of Persons with Disabilities' (21 January 2020), www.equalityhumanrights.com/en/our-human-rights-work/monitoring-and-promoting-un-treaties/un-convention-rights-persons-disabilities.

[6] Nicholas Bamforth, Maleiha Malik and Colm O'Cinneide, *Discrimination Law: Theory and Context, Text and Materials* (Sweet & Maxwell 2008) 1098.

II. The Definition of Disability

Disability is defined in section 6(1) EqA 2010 as a 'physical or mental impairment that has a substantial and long-term adverse effect on [the disabled person's] ability to carry out normal day-to-day activities'.[7] There are four key questions to consider when determining whether an individual meets the definition of disability contained in section 6(1).[8] The first is whether the individual has a physical or mental impairment, which has to be considered in the context of 'its ordinary and natural meaning'.[9] Nonetheless, what is important is the *effect* of the impairment, and not its cause. What matters is not the cause of deafness,[10] but how it affects day-to-day communication. Indeed, the focus should be the impairment's effect on the individual's day-to-day activities.[11] It should also be long term, that is, has lasted at least 12 months, will last at least 12 months, or will last for the rest of the individual's life.

Being deaf is largely considered a long-term disability, an impairment for this purpose, in that it is a sensory 'loss' or lack of hearing which has a substantial and adverse effect on a deaf individual's ability to carry out day-to-day activities such as listening, communication, speaking, reading or writing. A search for any relevant case law that considers whether a deaf person meets the definition of disability was in vain, as was a search for any relevant case law that considered section 1 DDA 1995, which contained the previous definition of disability. This suggests that deaf claimants have generally not experienced any issues proving that they have a disability for the purposes of the DDA 1995 or the EqA 2010, although it is possible that this issue could have been considered at the first tier but not appealed.

Instead, we can turn to the House of Lords Select Committee on the Equality Act, which states that the EqA 2010 covers British Sign Language (BSL) signers because it imposes on service providers a legal obligation to make reasonable adjustments in communicating with them; and where BSL is their first or only language, these adjustments will very often be the provision of BSL interpreters.[12] Clearly this would not necessarily extend to deaf non-BSL signers, and the Royal National Institute of Deaf People advises that an individual who wears hearing aids may fit the definition, depending on the situation, but those with minor hearing loss are unlikely.[13]

The Disability Convention definition of disability is similar to the provisions on disability in the EqA 2010, and Article 1 is a 'crucial touchstone in understanding

[7] EqA 2010, s 6(1).

[8] *Goodwin v Patent Office* [1999] IRLR 4.

[9] *McNicol v Balfour Beatty* [2002] EWCA Civ 1074.

[10] *Walker v Sita Information Networking Computing Ltd* [2013] UKEAT/0097/12/KN.

[11] *J v DLA Piper UK LLP* [2010] UKEAT/0263/09/RN.

[12] House of Lords Select Committee on the Equality Act 2010 and Disability, 'The Equality Act 2010: The Impact on Disabled People' (Stationery Office Limited, 2016) HL Paper 117 para 55, https://publications.parliament.uk/pa/ld201516/ldselect/ldeqact/117/117.pdf.

[13] Royal National Institute for Deaf People, 'The Equality Act 2010' (16 March 2021), https://rnid.org.uk/information-and-support/your-rights/the-equality-act-2010.

the impact of the Disability Convention', evincing a predominantly social model of disability.[14] It defines persons with disabilities as those 'who have long-term physical, mental, intellectual or sensory impairments which in interaction with various barriers may hinder their full and effective participation in society on an equal basis with others'.

Jurisprudence emanating from the United Nations Committee on the Rights of Persons with Disabilities ('the Committee') provides insight into how deaf individuals who have submitted complaints to the Committee have met the definition of disability in Article 1. In *AM v Australia*[15] and *Beasley v Australia*,[16] the complainant was deaf and required Australian Sign Language interpreting to communicate with others, and in *Lockrey v Australia*,[17] the complainant was deaf and required real-time steno-captioning of formal communications in order to communicate with others. It is clear from these three communications that a deaf signer and a deaf individual would fall within the auspices of the Article 1 definition within the Disability Convention.

III. Reasonable Adjustments

Reasonable adjustments, often referred to as 'accommodations' outside of the UK, are a facet of anti-discrimination law,[18] and described as the 'cornerstone of protection' for disabled people,[19] and 'key to the legislation'.[20] The duty to provide reasonable adjustments is a remedy for discrimination, one that works by requiring exceptions to the general norm instead of a change in the norm itself.[21] Reasonable adjustments involve a measure of substantive equality. Baroness Hale explained that reasonable adjustments are considered to be *more* favourable treatment.[22]

The failure to comply with any one of the two reasonable adjustment duties amounts to discrimination against a disabled person to whom the duty is owed. These requirements fall into two categories: reactive duties in employment, and anticipatory duties which require service providers and persons exercising public functions to take proactive steps to make their services accessible.[23] There are a number of hurdles to overcome before the duty to make reasonable adjustments is even trigged: the identification of a policy, criterion or practice,[24] a physical

[14] Sarah Fraser Butlin, 'The UN Convention on the Rights of Persons with Disabilities: Does the Equality Act 2010 Measure up to UK International Commitments?' (2011) 40 *Industrial Law Journal* 432.

[15] *AM v Australia* [2015] UN Doc CRPDC13D122013.

[16] *Beasley v Australia* [2016] CRPD/C/15/D/13/2013.

[17] *Lockrey v Australia* [2016] CRPD/C/15/D/13/2013.

[18] Tarunath Khaitan, *A Theory of Discrimination Law* (Oxford University Press, 2014) 76.

[19] Bob Hepple, *Equality: The Legal Framework*, 2nd edn (Hart Publishing, 2014) 94.

[20] Michael Connolly, *Townshend-Smith on Discrimination Law: Text, Cases and Materials* (Cavendish Publishing, 2004) 76.

[21] Khaitan (n 18) 77–78.

[22] *Archibald v Fife Council* [2004] UKHL 32 [47].

[23] Connolly (n 20) 95–96.

[24] EqA 2010, s 20(3).

feature,[25] or an auxiliary aid,[26] followed by a comparison exercise[27] and the need to show a substantive disadvantage if the requirement is not provided for.

Once the necessary adjustments are identified, the remaining question to answer is whether that adjustment is a reasonable one to be made in the circumstances, and this is a limit to the accommodation that can be sought.[28] Burns and Sen Gupta argue that the key to reasonableness can be found in two concepts: practicality and effectiveness.[29] The reasonable step must be practical to take, both in terms of feasibility and resources, and the more effective a step will be to take, the more reasonable it will be to take it.[30] However, an adjustment that provides only partial assistance is much less likely to be construed as reasonable, and therefore will not qualify as a reasonable adjustment.[31]

While deaf individuals have a legal right to seek reasonable adjustments, they are often not put in place, affirming discrimination and disadvantage. This is because it requires a liberal interpretation of the law to be effective. Instead, it is largely restrictive. The body of case law is limited to just five cases when examining legal jurisprudence for references to deaf individuals: the arrest of a profoundly deaf claimant without an interpreter, unsuccessful as he had been able to sell cannabis to undercover officers without an interpreter (*Finnigan v Northumbria Police Chief Constable*);[32] a policy to use screened rooms for interview, and offhand, disrespectful treatment (*Appleby v Department for Work and Pensions*);[33] unfairly applied criteria for redundancy selection and the manner of dismissal (*Berry v GB Electronics Ltd*);[34] the court, local authority and the Children and Family Court Advisory and Support Service's (CAFCASS) duty to provide the right level of support to parents in determining the care and placement for adoption orders (*Re C (A Child) (Care Proceedings: Deaf Parent)*);[35] and the provision of an interpreter for live concerts (*Reynolds, Nelson & Cassandro v Live in the UK Ltd*).[36]

A. Single, One-off Adjustments

An interesting observation regarding the first four cases aforementioned – *Finnigan*, *Appleby*, *Berry* and *Reynolds* – is that the reasonable adjustments required tended to be of a single, one-off, nature, that is, during an arrest, a visit

[25] EqA 2010, s 20(4).
[26] EqA 2010, s 20(5).
[27] EqA 2010, ss 13(1) and 20(3).
[28] Khaitan (n 18) 76.
[29] Andrew Burns and Diya Sen Gupta, 'Reasonable Adjustments: The Way Forward' (2004) 154 *New Law Journal* 452.
[30] ibid.
[31] ibid.
[32] [2013] EWCA Civ 1191 (Court of Appeal).
[33] [2003] CLY 2083 (County Court).
[34] [2000] EAT/0882/00 (Employment Appeal Tribunal).
[35] [2014] EWCA Civ 128 (Court of Appeal).
[36] [2021] E89YJ500 Cty Court.

to the jobcentre and a redundancy meeting. The fourth case, *Re C*, was about the provision of support by the court, local authority and CAFCASS to parents subjected to childcare proceedings, which is slightly different as any such reasonable adjustments would have been required on an intermittent basis rather than once, but they would nevertheless be a series of one-off adjustments.

Meager and others conducted a study which confirmed that one-off or initial costs were much more likely to be incurred than ongoing/recurrent costs, and that approximately four-fifths of establishments incurring a cost when making these types of adjustments had incurred only initial costs when introducing the changes.[37] Conversely, ongoing and recurrent costs were most likely to be incurred by establishments making adjustments for concessionary purposes, home delivery, and specific help, as well as those providing sign language interpretation and audio tapes.[38] The Business Disability Forum states that the average cost of a reasonable adjustment is £75,[39] and Acas confirms that many adjustments will be simple and affordable.[40] In many cases, a significant proportion reported that no costs were incurred, and these cases have been included in the average cost calculations with a value of zero, and where a cost was incurred, respondents were unable to estimate it.[41]

To support Meager and others' theory, a search of cases that considered various reasonable adjustments revealed that the majority of the adjustments were ones where no or minimal costs were incurred, such as not allowing a dyslexic employee to give her account without reference and assistance from accompanying notes but from her memory alone in a disciplinary hearing,[42] extending a time limit for an appeal against dismissal,[43] and providing hardware and IT software or transferring the claimant to an alternative role.[44] In addition, adjustments made by the respondent included a magnifying glass, a large key telephone, adjusted duties such as reading emails, adjusted hours of 10am to 4pm, and amended absence trigger points under the employer's attendance management policy.[45] Covering the costs of private psychiatric services and counselling triggered by work-related stress was too a reasonable adjustment.[46] Written instructions, a well-structured work environment, clarifying aspects of a job and explaining etiquette and the

[37] Nigel Meager and others, 'Costs and Benefits to Service Providers of Making Reasonable Adjustments under Part III of the Disability Discrimination Act' (Institute for Employment Studies, 2002) Research Report No 169, 86, www.researchgate.net/profile/Nigel_Meager/publication/269101724_Costs_and_benefits_to_service_providers_of_making_reasonable_adjustments_under_Part_III_of_the_Disability_Discrimination_Act/links/5480652f0cf25b80dd71f6c2.pdf.

[38] ibid 87.

[39] Business Disability Forum, 'Reasonable Adjustments - What They Are and Why They Are Important' (11 September 2024), https://businessdisabilityforum.org.uk/resource/reasonable-adjustments-smes.

[40] Acas, 'Reasonable Adjustments at Work: What Reasonable Adjustments Are' (30 January 2025), www.acas.org.uk/reasonable-adjustments.

[41] Meager and others (n 37) 88.

[42] *Emmens v Molnlycke Healthcare Limited* [2016] WL 05335357 [2].

[43] *Fox (Deceased) v British Airways plc* [2015] Employment Appeal Tribunal WL 1786103.

[44] *Cherrington v Home Office* [2015] WL 12591134 (Employment Tribunal).

[45] ibid 48.

[46] *Croft Vets Ltd v Butcher* [2013] EqLR 1170.

unwritten rules of the workplace, and awareness training, were also all accepted as reasonable adjustments in respect of an employee with Asperger's syndrome.[47]

To transplant these reasonable adjustments into a deaf context, it could be suggested that allowing a deaf employee to give their account through BSL in a disciplinary hearing, allowing a deaf employee more time to appeal against dismissal due to language barriers, allowing a BSL-English interpreter to translate emails into BSL, amending hours to suit BSL-English interpreter availability, and ignoring deaf-related absences, such as for audiology appointments, providing instructions in writing, explaining etiquette and unwritten rules, and deaf awareness training, could all be considered reasonable adjustments.

B. Recurrent Adjustments

There is only one case with a deaf claimant relevant to the provision of interpreters as a recurrent adjustment. An on-platform interpreter for COVID-19 briefings – that is, next to or in the same frame as the speaker, usually a minister of state or Public Health England official – was not reasonable in the circumstances as provision had been made on the BBC News channel.[48] We therefore need to consider other cases that involved auxiliary aids to gain a better picture. An emergency personal assistant for a barrister with multiple sclerosis was considered a reasonable adjustment.[49] Although the costs involved are unknown, this case suggests that the Crown Prosecution Service provided and presumably funded the provision of personal assistants for a disabled employee. The provision of a workplace buddy to read aloud emails, database and input data was also considered reasonable.[50]

In terms of ongoing, higher-cost adjustments, there is some ambiguity on what would now constitute a reasonable adjustment following the Employment Appeal Tribunal's decision that there is a cap on the costs an employer is expected to pay for adjustments.[51] In this case, £250,000 per year for lipspeakers[52] to accompany a deaf diplomat in Kazakhstan was unreasonable. In contrast, the Court of Appeal determined that an adjustment costing £200,000 to install a wheelchair access at a branch was reasonable,[53] presumably because this would have been a one-off adjustment. One can also surmise that the adjustments in *Tooley* may have been considered reasonable as they can be fulfilled by the utilisation of individuals paid

[47] *Fotheringham v Perth & Kinross* [2013] WL 12111408 (Employment Tribunal) [249].

[48] *R (on the application of Katherine Rowley) v Minister for the Cabinet Office* [2021] EWHC 2108 Admin.

[49] *Tooley v Crown Prosecution Service* [2016] WL 05335328 (Employment Tribunal) [189].

[50] *Cherrington v Home Office* (n 44) [12a].

[51] *Cordell v Foreign and Commonwealth Office* [2011] UKEAT/0016/11/SM (Employment Appeal Tribunal).

[52] A lipspeaker is a hearing person who has been professionally trained to be easy to lipread. Association of Lipspeakers, 'Association of Lipspeakers (ALS): Spoken Words Made Visible' (2024), www.lipspeaking.co.uk.

[53] *Royal Bank of Scotland Group Plc v Allen* [2009] EWCA Civ 1213.

the minimum wage (provided they receive the appropriate training), rather than specialist support such as BSL-English interpreters, lipspeakers and Palantypists.

The recurrent adjustments required in the former case were not considered to be reasonable, and a precedent has now been set: a recurrent cost of £250,000 per year is too high to be considered a reasonable adjustment. The implication is that if a deaf employee seeks promotion or a new role where comparable support cannot be guaranteed, the adjustment may be deemed unreasonable. This creates, in effect, a 'glass ceiling',[54] a structural limit that reflects the Deaf Legal Illusion: that opportunity is formally open to all, but in practice, mediated by cost-based exclusions. This case also serves as a reminder that the provision of adjustments for deaf people can be expensive.

One of the rare instances where a deaf claimant succeeded in securing recurrent adjustments involved a school pupil who required ongoing BSL support, a Teacher of the Deaf Children and Young People (ToD), and access to a deaf base.[55] The Health and Education Chamber's decision hinged not on cost, but on whose understanding of deafness it accepted: the authority's audiological model or the pupil's lived experience, supported by a culturally informed expert. The tribunal chose the latter. BSL support was the auxiliary aid, and the claimant suffered a substantive disadvantage by the failure to provide BSL and ToD support, the impact on the claimant's mental and physical health, the denial of the opportunity for full multi-modal learning, isolation in their learning, and not able to access the school's deaf base to interact with other deaf learners and peers. The Chamber confirmed that the claimant belongs to a linguistic and cultural minority under Article 30 of the United Nations Convention for the Rights of the Child[56] and Article 24 of the Disability Rights Convention which confers a duty to facilitate the learning of sign language and the promotion of the linguistic identity of the deaf community.

These decisions, and the distinction between one-off and recurrent adjustments, illustrate one aspect of the Deaf Legal Illusion: although the reasonable adjustment duty appears to offer a route for redress, its application often turns on narrow financial or procedural interpretations that fail to account for deaf people's ongoing needs.

C. Infringements of Human Rights

There have been a number of attempts to develop Convention jurisprudence in relation to deaf people. When a deaf man died in police custody after sustaining serious head injuries in a fall down some stairs, the police had violated Article 2

[54] The existence of a glass ceiling implies that gender (or other) disadvantages are stronger at the top of the hierarchy than at lower levels and that those disadvantages become worse later in a person's career. David A Cotter and others, 'The Glass Ceiling Effect' (2001) 80 *Social Forces* 655, 655.

[55] *Braid v Fife Council* FTS/HEC/AC/23/0197 (Health and Education Chamber).

[56] United Nations, Convention on the Rights of the Child E/CN.4/RES/1990/74 (1990).

because they did not provide him with a pen and paper to enable him to communicate his concerns about his state of health.[57] There was a violation of Articles 3 and 5 when the authorities did not take measures to accommodate a deaf man with learning difficulties within a reasonable time and did not take reasonable steps to enable him to challenge his detention in prison for almost three months.[58] There was a violation of Article 8 as the Polish authorities had failed to envisage measures in relation to a deaf man's contact rights with his son, including obtaining expert evidence from specialists familiar with the problems faced by deaf people, and focusing on the communication barrier between father and son instead of reflecting on the possible means of overcoming it.[59]

These three cases illustrate a simple fact: if a deaf individual's human rights are infringed due to the failure to make adjustments, the adjustments are more likely to be considered reasonable. In essence, adjustments are more readily deemed necessary where fundamental human rights are under threat, such as in the case of the right to liberty and security of person, and the right to respect for private and family life. This compounds the Deaf Legal Illusion. In some situations, where it is only the lack of adjustments at play, the law perpetuates the impression that the deaf individual will be protected and can expect adjustments to be made. While this expectation often collapses without a parallel threat to core rights, the dynamic shifts when the absence of adjustments directly causes a human rights infringement.

These rare instances, whether a successful claim for recurrent BSL support, or a finding of human rights infringement, do not disprove the Deaf Legal Illusion. Rather, they expose its fragility: legal recognition is contingent on exceptional circumstances, not a consistent duty to accommodate deaf people's lived realities.

IV. Equality Duties and Monitoring

A. Public Sector Equality Duties

The public sector equality duty (PSED) is in sections 149–157 EqA 2010. The aim of these sections is to make the promotion of equality on all the equality grounds central to the work of public authorities so that they take account of equality in the day-to-day work of policymaking, service delivery, employment practice and other functions.[60] The PSED has been described as an 'integral and important part of the mechanisms for ensuring the fulfilment of the aims of anti-discrimination

[57] *Jasinskis v Latvia* [2010] App No 4574408 (ECtHR).

[58] *ZH v Hungary* [2012] App No 2897311 (ECtHR).

[59] *Kacper Nowakowski v Poland* [2017] App No 3240713 (ECtHR); European Court of Human Rights, 'Factsheet - Persons with Disabilities and the European Convention on Human Rights' (2024), www.echr.coe.int/documents/d/echr/FS_Disabled_ENG.

[60] Simonetta Manfredi, Lucy Vickers and Kate Clayton-Hathway, 'The Public Sector Equality Duty: Enforcing Equality Rights Through Second-Generation Regulation' (2018) 47 *Industrial Law Journal* 365, 367.

legislation',[61] its aim being to 'integrate consideration of advancement of equality into the day-to-day business of all bodies subject to the duty'.[62] One of the initial attractions of the duties was their potential to offer an alternative pathway to achieving equality that could run in tandem with the well-established individual litigation approach.[63] Indeed, Bell suggests that the equality duties could 'escape the narrow confines'[64] of the individual enforcement model, discussed below.

In practice, the EqA 2010 provides that public authorities, and those who exercise public functions, must have 'due regard'[65] to the need to eliminate discrimination and other conduct prohibited by the Act,[66] advance equality of opportunity,[67] and foster good relations.[68] The EqA 2010 sets out how those aims of the PSED can be met, and explains that the advancement of equality of opportunity can be achieved by removing or minimising disadvantage suffered by groups of individuals, taking steps to meet the needs of groups of individuals, and encouraging participation in public life.[69] The fostering of good relations can be achieved by tackling prejudice and promoting understanding.[70] Section 149(6) goes on to suggest that complying with these aims may involve treating some persons more favourably than others.

Although cases are few, the measure of success of the PSED is not so much via law reports, but through the development of a culture of mainstreaming equality measures in public sector organisations. There is evidence to suggest that implementation in practice is limited, with the criticism focused on the fact that many organisations have developed bureaucratic processes to ensure compliance with the duty, rather than focusing on removing the inequality in question. In effect, a 'tick box' mentality has developed, focusing on procedures for decision-making. This enables public bodies to show that they have considered equality issues, rather than focusing on the impact of decisions made, and whether they have been altered to ensure that equality issues are properly addressed.[71] Nonetheless, despite its shortcomings, it is argued that the PSED is an example of transformative equality, a point supported by Hepple.[72]

[61] *R (Elias) v Secretary for State for Defence* [2006] EWCA Civ 1293 [274] as cited in *Bracking and others v Secretary of State for Work and Pensions (Bracking)* [2013] EWCA Civ 1345 [26].

[62] Equality and Human Rights Commission, 'Technical Guidance on the Public Sector Equality Duty: England | EHRC' (2023) para 2.10, www.equalityhumanrights.com/guidance/public-sector-equality-duty/technical-guidance-public-sector-equality-duty-england-0#document-download.

[63] Mark Bell, 'Judicial Enforcement of the Duties on Public Authorities to Promote Equality' [2010] *Public Law* 672, 673.

[64] ibid.

[65] These duties were identified in *R (Brown) v Secretary of State for Work and Pensions* [2008] EWHC 3158 (High Court), known as the '*Brown* principles', and added to by *Bracking*.

[66] EqA 2010, s 149(1)(a).

[67] EqA 2010, s 149(1)(b).

[68] EqA 2010, s 149(1)(c).

[69] EqA 2010, s 149(3).

[70] EqA 2010, s 149(5).

[71] Lucy Vickers, 'Promoting Equality or Fostering Resentment? The Public Sector Equality Duty and Religion and Belief' (2011) 31 *Legal Studies* 135, 137.

[72] Hepple (n 19) 18.

Section 156 EqA 2010 prevents private law claims from being brought in respect of any failure to perform the general duties, although such a breach may be relevant by way of the evidential background to a discrimination claim under the Act.[73] Otherwise, alleged breaches of the PSED are enforceable by way of judicial review proceedings. The specific duties can only be challenged by the Equality and Human Rights Commission (EHRC),[74] which can assess compliance of both general and specific duties and Schedule 2 Equality Act 2006 sets out the rules for carrying out such assessments. Where it identifies non-compliance with equality obligations, the EHRC can issue a compliance notice requiring compliance with the relevant duty, and if the public authority does not, the EHRC may apply to the court for an order requiring the body to comply.[75]

A search for PSED-related cases that include deaf people has not proved particularly fruitful. It was argued that the Department for Work and Pensions' (DWP) limit on the amount of certain payments made under the Access to Work scheme was unlawful because it constituted a breach of the DWP's PSED.[76] This was rejected by Kerr J on the basis that 'a decision on how to allocate resources as between different categories of persons sharing the same protected characteristic (albeit in different ways) was always likely to be an ambitious target for an allegation of breach of the equality duty'.[77] The DWP had failed to comply with its PSED over a period of years, but the claim for judicial review was dismissed as the DWP had offered the claimant a reasonable system of communication.[78]

Upon a wider search of relevant case law, however, there appear to be two recurrent themes in recent PSED case law: firstly, the failure of public authorities to provide proper evidence of compliance with the PSED, which is likely to lead to a finding of a breach of the duty, and secondly, the failure of public authorities to provide evidence that all relevant protected characteristics have been considered.[79]

Some case studies provided by the EHRC provide examples of how the PSED can work in practice, thus demonstrating its transformative potential. Tower Hamlets Council used its PSED to improve the educational attainment of its pupils

[73] Lexis+ UK Practical Guidance, 'Practice Note - Public Sector Equality Duty', https://plus.lexis.com/uk/practical-guidance-uk/public-sector-equality-duty.

[74] John Wadham and others (eds), *Blackstone's Guide to the Equality Act 2010*, 3rd edn (Oxford University Press, 2016) 167.

[75] Lexis+ UK Practical Guidance (n 73).

[76] *R (Buxton) v Secretary of State for Work and Pensions [2018]* [2018] EWHC 2196 Admin (High Court) [1].

[77] ibid [78].

[78] *R (on the application of Atherton) v Secretary of State for Work and Pensions* [2019] High Court EWHC 395 (Admin) [108].

[79] Claire Darwin, 'The Public Sector Equality Duty: An Update and Overview' (Matrix Chambers, 29 January 2016) para 12, www.matrixlaw.co.uk/wp-content/uploads/2016/03/27_01_2016_12_40_30_Public-Sector-Equality-Duty-Update-and-OverviewvP.pdf, referring to the cases of *R (Cushnie) v Secretary of State for Health* [2014] EWHC 3626 (Admin), [2015] PTSR 384, *R (Winder) v Sandwell Metropolitan Borough Council* [2014] EWHC 2617 and *R (Fakih) v Secretary of State for the Home Department* [2014] UKUT 513.

from eight per cent achieving five or more grades A–C at GCSE in 1990 to 62 per cent in 2012 by identifying that the majority of underperforming students came from homes where English was not the first language, and took the necessary steps to address that.[80] Thames Valley Police implemented an 18-month programme to reduce police use of stop and search powers (Black people being up to six times more likely to be stopped and searched than white people). This included a revised policy, training for all officers and detailed statistical monitoring of stop and search patterns and resulted in a reduction to 3.2 per cent of the stop and search of Black individuals.[81] The PSED has also seen an improvement in decision-making and transparency by public authorities, and efforts to mainstream equality in an organisation's culture.[82]

A report revealed that the public authorities that successfully implemented the duty demonstrated a number of factors in common.[83] These included: visible, committed, and coordinated leadership; appointed 'champions' or dedicated officers with equalities expertise; consultation and engagement with service users; and data collection and monitoring to form a strong evidence base.[84] The same report does mention deaf people. The PSED led to the adaptation of hospital wards and deaf awareness training for staff alongside a new intercom system for deaf patients to access wards.[85] An independent evaluation of the NHS Equality Delivery System conducted in 2012[86] also showed early evidence of improvement in engagement with local voluntary and community organisations and patient groups, including deaf people. There was also evidence of increased knowledge and awareness of equality with staff at all levels.[87]

All in all, the case studies put forward to demonstrate how the PSED can and does work in practice supports the contention that the PSED is potentially transformative, as it has the wherewithal to effect positive changes in society either through the decision-making process of public authorities, increased consultation and engagement with employees and service users, and the gathering of data in order to substantiate the claims of inequality by marginalised groups. While the PSED aspires to transformation, however, its procedural limitations mean that, for deaf people, its promise often remains part of the broader illusion of legal inclusion.

[80] Robert Brian Wilks, 'Making Equality Law Work for Deaf People' (Doctoral Dissertation, University of Leicester, 2019) 177–78.

[81] ibid 178.

[82] ibid.

[83] Kate Clayton-Hathway, 'The Public Sector Equality Duty - Analysis of Supporting Evidence' (Oxford Brookes Centre for Diversity Policy Research and Practice, 2013) 15.

[84] ibid.

[85] ibid 8; see also Elizabeth Sclater, 'Making Practice Happen: Practitioners' Views on the Most Effective Specific Equality Duties' (Equality and Human Rights Commission, 2009) 28, www.edf.org.uk/wp-content/uploads/2009/02/final-report-making-practice-happen.pdf.

[86] Shared Intelligence, 'Evaluation of the Equality Delivery System for the NHS - Phase One: Final Report' (University Hospitals Birmingham NHS Foundation Trust, 2012) para 4.10, www.uhb.nhs.uk/Downloads/pdf/EdsEvaluationPhaseOneFinalReport.pdf.

[87] Clayton-Hathway (n 83) 8.

B. State Reporting

The Disability Convention requires governments to designate one or more 'independent mechanisms' to 'promote, protect and monitor implementation' of the Human Rights Convention, and the EHRC has been designated a member of the UK's Independent Mechanism. The Disability Convention was given legal effect in the UK in 2011,[88] and while this was repealed by the European Union (Withdrawal) Act 2018, it has been subsumed into domestic law following the UK's exit from the European Union.[89]

In the UK, the Office for Disability Issues takes the lead in coordinating the UK's state report to the Disability Convention, securing contributions from the devolved administrations, which are responsible for implementing the Disability Convention in their jurisdictions.[90] In relation to such reports, Keith[91] and Donnelly[92] argue that these reports often exaggerate the degree of compliance. In support of this argument, the Committee's review of the UK's first Initial Report,[93] which describes how the Disability Convention is being implemented in the UK, resulted in 60 recommendations for the UK Government to bring it closer to implementation of the Disability Convention.[94]

The BDA commented: 'the Committee . . . condemned the UK Government's attempts to misrepresent impact through unanswered questions, misused statistics and a smokescreen of statements on policies and legislation which fail to implement the rights of deaf and disabled people'.[95] In response, the UK Government denied the Committee's findings: 'We're disappointed that this report does not accurately reflect the evidence we gave to the UN, and fails to recognise all the progress we've made to empower disabled people in all aspects of their lives'.[96] This response echoes the general approach the Government appears to have taken to the Disability Convention.

[88] European Communities (Definition of Treaties) (United Nations Convention on the Rights of Persons with Disabilities) Order 2009/1181.

[89] European Union (Withdrawal) Act 2018, s 4(1).

[90] Office for Disability Issues, 'UK Initial Report: On the UN Convention on the Rights of Persons with Disabilities' (Office for Disability Issues, 2011) para 348, assets.publishing.service.gov.uk/media/5a7ead1b40f0b6230268ad22/uk-initial-report.pdf.

[91] Linda Camp Keith, 'The United Nations International Covenant on Civil and Political Rights: Does It Make a Difference in Human Rights Behavior?' (1999) 36 *Journal of Peace Research* 95, 98.

[92] Jack Donnelly, *Universal Human Rights in Theory and Practice* (Cornell University Press, 2013) 173.

[93] United Nations, 'Consideration of Reports Submitted by States Parties under Article 35 of the Convention. Initial Reports of States Parties Due in 2011: United Kingdom of Great Britain and Northern Ireland' (CRPD Committee, 2011) UN Doc CRPD/C/GBR/1.

[94] Office of the High Commissioner for Human Rights, 'Committee on the Rights of Persons with Disabilities Reviews Report of the United Kingdom: Country Review' (24 August 2017, www.ohchr.org/en/press-releases/2017/08/committee-rights-persons-disabilities-reviews-report-united-kingdom.

[95] British Deaf Association, 'UN Committee Paves the Way for a BSL Act – British Deaf Association' (31 August 2017), https://bda.org.uk/press-release-uncrpd-bsl.

[96] Mike Lambert, 'Austerity Has Trampled over Disabled People's Rights. But the UK Won't Admit It' (*The Guardian*, 4 September 2017), www.theguardian.com/commentisfree/2017/sep/04/austerity-disabled-people-rights-uk-un-government.

The UK's follow-up report to the Committee[97] charts a familiar pattern: polished assertions of progress, selective statistics, and an enduring reluctance to grapple with the structural inequalities that deaf and disabled people continue to face. The tone is technocratic rather than transformative. Like the first report, it reads more as an exercise in defence than accountability. At its core, the report seeks to demonstrate that the UK has responded appropriately to the Committee's 2016 inquiry, which found evidence of 'grave or systematic violations' of Convention rights.[98] But rather than engage with the substance of those findings, the UK Government continues to lean heavily on generalities. It points to cumulative distributional analyses in fiscal statements and consultations on social care reform. It claims compliance through process: the existence of the PSED, the publication of the Disability Green Paper, the intention to legislate at some future point. Yet these measures, while not insignificant, fall short of what the Disability Convention demands: a rights-based, participatory, and evaluative approach to policymaking.

In terms of deaf people, the 2022 report[99] offers limited engagement. It references the BSL Act 2022, recognising BSL as a language of Great Britain and outlining duties on the UK Government to promote its use. It also notes the creation of a BSL Advisory Board and the use of BSL videos in government communications. While these developments are welcome, there is no mention of accessible services in health, education, and public life. This once again highlights the Deaf Legal Illusion: that deaf people are covered, when in fact they are largely invisible.

Taken together, the UK's PSED and state reporting practice illustrate a central feature of the Deaf Legal Illusion. The mechanisms for inclusive policymaking and international monitoring exist. So too do the obligations. But in the absence of enforceable duties or meaningful engagement with the communities affected, these processes become just another layer of symbolic compliance: legal forms without legal force.

V. Enforcement

In order to assess the effectiveness of the law, consideration should be given to the enforcement mechanisms available to deaf individuals to challenge discrimination or other infringements of their rights under the law. It is worth bearing in mind that the most common mechanism of doing so is by way of the individual enforcement model. Equality law is primarily concerned with prohibiting discrimination and providing individuals who experience discrimination with a remedy. The law is concerned only with that individual instance of behaviour, which means the outcome does not affect other individuals or change societal structures. It is

[97] UK Government, 'The UK's 2022 Follow-up Report to the 2016 Inquiry by the UN Committee on the Rights of Persons with Disabilities' (2022), https://assets.publishing.service.gov.uk/media/639b0a96e90e072182dffe8f/FINAL_Web-Accessible_UK_2022_follow-up_inquiry_report_UNCRPD.pdf.

[98] CRPD Committee, 'Inquiry Concerning the United Kingdom of Great Britain and Northern Ireland Carried out by the Committee under Article 6 of the Optional Protocol to the Convention: Report of the Committee' (2017) CRPD/C/15/4.

[99] UK Government (n 97).

reactive rather than proactive, negative rather than positive, and continues to meet O'Cinneide's description of this type of antidiscrimination law:[100] the individual enforcement model relies excessively on an approach that resembles sending a fire engine to fight a fire rather than preventing that fire in the first place.[101]

A. The Human Rights Convention

The Convention's falling grace is that for groups such as deaf people, while it contains a complementary right in Article 14 to non-discrimination on the grounds of status in the exercise of Convention rights, it is not a standalone right but operates in connection with other rights, meaning it can be used to challenge discriminatory treatment only where another Convention right is also engaged. Lawson confirms that the concept of discrimination that has emerged from Article 14 cases is narrow and has not yet offered a great deal of assistance to disabled people[102] in challenging oppression.

It is also worth noting that only public authorities can be sued directly under the HRA 1998.[103] The Human Rights Convention itself places obligations on states, not private individuals or organisations.[104] This significantly limits its usefulness for deaf people, who are more likely to experience barriers in private sector contexts such as employment, housing, or service provision, where Convention rights may still be relevant but cannot be directly enforced.

It is clear that only a handful of judgments have been handed down by the European Court of Human Rights (ECtHR) in relation to disabled people. Clements and Read contend that:

> [T]he reason for the dearth of such cases at the Court can be placed at the door of the usual culprits; the physical, social and economic barriers that prevent disabled people from exercising their rights. Some of these barriers to access are embedded in the circumstances in which many disabled people live their lives. Some are related to the unresponsiveness of the law, the judiciary and the practicalities of enforcement mechanisms to the needs and rights of disabled people. Other barriers reside within the judicial process itself.[105]

[100] Dominique Allen, 'Rethinking the Australian Model of Promoting Gender Equality' in Katharine G Young and Kim Rubenstein (eds), *The Public Law of Gender: From the Local to the Global* (Cambridge University Press, 2016) 405.

[101] Colm O'Cinneide, 'Beyond the Limits of Equal Treatment: The Use of Positive Duties in Equality Law' (Mainstreaming Equality: Models for a Statutory Duty, Equality Authority, Dublin, Ireland, 27 February 2003) 21.

[102] Anna Lawson, 'The EU Rights Based Approach to Disability: Strategies for Shaping an Inclusive Society' (2005) 6 *International Journal of Discrimination and the Law* 269, 275.

[103] Human Rights Act 1998, s 6.

[104] Convention for the Protection of Human Rights and Fundamental Freedoms, Art 1.

[105] Luke Clements and Janet Read, 'The Dog That Didn't Bark: The Issue of Access under the European Convention on Human Rights by Disabled People' in Anna Lawson and Caroline Gooding (eds), *Disability Rights in Europe: from theory to practice* (Hart Publishing, 2005) 23–24.

Clements and Read further argue that the fact that the ECtHR continues to have profound difficulty in identifying and addressing state responsibility for discrimination against disabled people is 'a failure of imagination, and a failure of the advocates and judges to find new ways of expressing the language of the Human Rights Convention'.[106] This is attributed to a number of factors. Firstly, the judicial misconception that somehow human rights are not seen as relevant to disabled people, due to a tendency to regard disabled people as 'other', placing them in a separate category.[107] Secondly, disabled people are often viewed primarily as recipients of health and welfare services rather than citizens with the same rights as others, a factor that is generally unique to disabled people.[108] Seem familiar?

Thirdly, the language of the Human Rights Convention does not provide the wherewithal for allowing Strasbourg to 'identify and address state responsibility for discrimination against disabled people'.[109] In particular, the fact that Article 14 of the Human Rights Convention (the prohibition of discrimination) does not specifically mention disability shows a lack of vision on the part of the drafters.[110] The Convention is similarly silent on the rights of children and gay and lesbian people, but this has not prevented the ECtHR developing jurisprudence which identifies, articulates and attempts to justify the injustice they experience.[111] Fourthly, the plight of disabled people is not considered to be 'fashionable'. The ECtHR has challenged established modes of communication, requiring the language of human rights to be used in the domains of women, racial minorities, and gay and lesbian people in new ways to accommodate new paradigms and create new conceptual vehicles.[112] Instead, emphasis tends to be on the discrimination faced by disabled people rather than their civil and human rights.[113]

The possibility of the Human Rights Convention providing clear-cut answers to all legal and ethical questions related to deaf people is subject to limitations,[114] as it does not even mention disability as a protected ground and does not contain any requirements on public authorities to take affirmative action, nor does it impose any positive duties. Deaf people are generally unable to seek redress for inequalities or lack of access such as failing to be provided with a sign language interpreter, unless one of the absolute rights under the Human Rights Convention has also been infringed. In short, the Human Rights Convention is a further example of the formal equality paradigm. These issues also reflect a recurring feature of the Deaf Legal Illusion: the appearance of protection without full or practical coverage.

[106] ibid 28.
[107] ibid 26.
[108] ibid.
[109] ibid 28.
[110] ibid.
[111] ibid.
[112] ibid 27.
[113] ibid.
[114] Aart Hendriks and Theresia Degener, 'The Evolution of a European Perspective on Disability Legislation' (1994) 1 *European Journal of Health Law* 343, 361.

B. The Disability Convention

The UK Government has ratified the Disability Convention's Optional Protocol, which enables people with disabilities to make a complaint to the Committee if they believe that their Convention rights have been breached, that is, they have been oppressed, although they do have to exhaust means of redress via the UK before doing so. The quasi-judicial Committee charged with receiving complaints under the treaty consists of experts who evaluate the merits of 'communications' and issue 'views' as to whether the state party in question violated its treaty commitment.[115] The Optional Protocol also gives the Committee authority to undertake inquiries, when reliable information is received into allegations of grave or systematic violations of Convention rights. Nonetheless, Cole argues that the individual complaints procedures will have a larger impact on human rights practices when compared with interstate complaints mechanisms as the latter have never been used and hence do not pose a credible threat to rights-abusing countries due to 'sovereignty costs'.[116]

In contrast, individuals are less concerned about upholding sovereignty norms and thus more likely to file complaints,[117] although this remains to be seen as only 59 complaints have been registered under the Disability Convention to date. Nineteen have been closed, and 40 are pending.[118] If the Committee decides that the facts before it disclose a violation by the state party of the complainant's rights under the treaty, it invites the state party to supply information within 180 days on the steps it has taken to give effect to its findings and recommendations. The state's response is then transmitted to the complainant for comments. If the state party fails to take appropriate action, the case is kept under consideration by the Committee under the follow-up procedure. A dialogue is thus pursued with the state party and the case remains open until satisfactory measures are taken. All information related to this aspect of the procedure is not confidential and will thus be available for public consumption.[119] Following the Committee's recommendations, state parties are then required to submit a written response to the communication within six months, including any information on any action taken in the light of the views and recommendations of the Committee.[120]

[115] Wade M Cole, 'Human Rights as Myth and Ceremony? Reevaluating the Effectiveness of Human Rights Treaties, 1981–2007 1' (2012) 117 *American Journal of Sociology* 1131, 1140.

[116] ibid 1141.

[117] ibid.

[118] CRPD Committee, 'Table of Pending Cases', www.ohchr.org/sites/default/files/documents/hrbodies/crpd/2022-09-23/Table_pending_cases_CRPD.xlsx; CRPD Committee, 'Follow up Table – Closed Cases', www.ohchr.org/sites/default/files/documents/hrbodies/crpd/FU-table-CRPD-cases.xlsx.

[119] United Nations, 'Individual Communications' (Office of the High Commissioner for Human Rights, 2025), www.ohchr.org/en/treaty-bodies/individual-communications.

[120] United Nations, 'Optional Protocol to the Convention on the Rights of Persons with Disabilities' (2006) A/RES/61/106, Art 5, www.ohchr.org/en/instruments-mechanisms/instruments/optional-protocol-convention-rights-persons-disabilities; United Nations, 'Rules of Procedure' (CRPD Committee 2016) UN Doc CRPD/C/1/Rev.1 r 75.

To date, only three communications are relevant to deaf people. While *AM*[121] was held to be inadmissible, *Lockrey*[122] and *Beasley*'s[123] communications were made in relation to the participation of deaf people in jury duty, whereupon they had been excluded from jury service as a result of needing an Auslan interpreter and real-time steno-captioning.[124] The Committee agreed with Ms Beasley and Mr Lockrey and found that Australia was in breach of its obligations under the Disability Convention,[125] particularly as Australia had argued that providing Auslan interpreters or steno-captioning affected the complexity, cost and duration of trials, yet 'it [did] not provide any data or analysis to demonstrate that it would constitute a disproportionate or undue burden'.[126] The Committee ordered Australia to take steps to compensate and reimburse Ms Beasley and Mr Lockrey for their legal costs, and also to take steps to permit them to participate in jury duty, and prevent the problem arising again.[127] Australia did not provide a written response,[128] and the position of deaf jurors in Australia remains unchanged.

The next question is: what complaints could deaf people make under the provisions of the Disability Convention? To answer this, I look to existing jurisprudence. Sweden failed to fulfil its obligations under the Disability Convention in rejecting the complainant's application for a building permit to build an indoor hydrotherapy pool at home to accommodate her disabilities, recommending that the state party reconsidered the application and provide adequate compensation.[129] Argentinian authorities kept a complainant in prison, requiring him to attend hospital appointments as an outpatient via ambulance transfers, posing a serious risk to his life and health, rather than as an inpatient, which was held to be in breach of the Disability Convention.[130] Hungary breached Articles 12 and 29 of the Disability Convention in respect of six complainants who had been removed from the electoral register and were unable to vote in the 2010 elections.[131]

Germany's model for the provision of integration subsidies did not effectively promote the employment of persons with reasonable adjustments as it tended to act as a deterrent for employers to employ individuals with disabilities due to its administrative complexities.[132] Austria failed to fulfil its obligations under

[121] *AM v Australia* (n 15).
[122] *Lockrey v Australia* (n 17).
[123] *Beasley v Australia* (n 16).
[124] RuleofLawInstitutePerson, 'Deaf Jurors and Discrimination' (Rule of Law Education Centre, 14 June 2016), www.ruleoflaw.org.au/deaf-jurors-and-discrimination.
[125] ibid.
[126] United Nations, 'Australia Violated Rights of Deaf People over Jury Service – UN Experts' (Office of the High Commissioner for Human Rights, 26 April 2016), www.ohchr.org/en/press-releases/2016/04/australia-violated-rights-deaf-people-over-jury-service-un-experts.
[127] ibid.
[128] Michael Lockrey [@mlockrey], 'Confirmation That Australia Has Not Provided a Written Response', x.com/mlockrey/status/1150948233880825856.
[129] *HM v Sweden* [2012] UN Doc CRPDC7D32011 [9.1].
[130] *Mr X v Argentina* [2014] UN Doc CRPDC11D82012.
[131] *Bujdosó and others v Hungary* [2013] UN Doc CRPDC10D42011.
[132] *Gröninger v Germany* [2014] UN Doc CRPDCD22010.

the Disability Convention as stops along a railway network did not have a digital audio system installed which reproduces the written text of the digital information displays for visually impaired individuals.[133] Finally, in Australia an individual with a mental and intellectual disability was detained without entering a plea of guilty or not guilty on the basis of his legal incapacity for 10 years and three months despite the fact that he would probably have been sentenced to a term of imprisonment not exceeding two to three years had he been convicted.[134]

If one was to extrapolate similar scenarios in respect of deaf people, one could surmise that if, for whatever reason, deaf individuals were under the guardianship of others and were denied the right to vote, this would be a contravention of the Disability Convention. The imprisonment of a deaf individual without providing that individual with the opportunity to enter a plea, and the lack of digital information displays where transport information was only available in audio format, could also be considered to be contraventions.

It is clear that the individual complaints procedure associated with the Disability Convention provides a source of redress for deaf people to challenge inequality, although this clearly has its limitations. Even when the Committee rules in favour of deaf complainants, the absence of enforceability perpetuates the Deaf Legal Illusion.

C. The Equality Act 2010

One way to assess the effectiveness of the EqA 2010 is through the lens of enforcement: how well does it enable deaf individuals to challenge the inequality they experience? There are three main routes: the employment tribunals for workplace discrimination claims, and the civil courts for discrimination claims against service providers, and judicial review for PSED-related claims. The statistics available fluctuate, and it is only possible to access disability discrimination claims for the employment tribunal. The civil courts only record claims within broader categories.

Between 2007 and 2012, the number of disability discrimination claims at the employment tribunal rose steadily, peaking at 7,676 in 2011/12, before collapsing following the introduction of employment tribunal fees in 2013.[135] After the Supreme Court abolished fees in 2017,[136] claims began to recover, reaching over 8,000 in 2019/20. While numbers remained high into 2022/23, figures for 2023/24 appear unusually low, likely reflecting reporting anomalies rather than a real decline.[137] It should be noted that this reporting does not disaggregate by

[133] *F v Austria* [2015] UN Doc CRPDC14D212014.

[134] *Noble v Australia* [2016] UN Doc CRPDC16D72012.

[135] Employment Appeal Tribunal Fees Order, SI 2013/1893.

[136] *R (on the application of UNISON) v Lord Chancellor* [2017] UKSC 51 (Supreme Court).

[137] GOV.UK, 'Tribunals Statistics Quarterly: October to December 2024' (13 March 2025), www.gov.uk/government/statistics/tribunals-statistics-quarterly-october-to-december-2024; GOV.UK, 'Tribunals Statistics Quarterly: July to September 2023' (14 December 2023), www.gov.uk/government/statistics/tribunals-statistics-quarterly-july-to-september-2023.

type of disability or by the nature of the discrimination claim. Although disability discrimination claims consistently outnumber those related to other protected characteristics, the success rate remains strikingly low: between 2019 and 2023, only two to three per cent of claims succeeded at hearing. The vast majority were withdrawn, struck out, or resolved through conciliation. These figures suggest that the individual enforcement model does little to address systemic disadvantage. For deaf claimants in particular the likelihood of securing a meaningful remedy remains small.

In practice, only around three to four per cent of all civil claims in England and Wales proceed to trial each year.[138] Applying this proportion to 'other non-money claims', a broad category that includes discrimination, family, and housing cases, the only statistics available, suggests that just a small fraction are ever adjudicated. For deaf claimants, many of whom pursue rights-based actions relating to inaccessible services in the county court, this represents a profound justice gap. Rights may exist in legislation, but the courtroom pathway to enforce them is functionally unavailable for most. This statistical attrition is emblematic of the Deaf Legal Illusion.

The total number of judicial review claims categorised as 'Civil – Other' has declined from over 2,100 in 2013 to fewer than 1,800 in 2024.[139] This category includes PSED-based challenges and other equality claims most likely to be brought by or on behalf of deaf people. Although these claims represent a crucial route for holding public authorities accountable, their shrinking frequency and the widening gap in case closure, just 49 per cent in 2024, highlight the growing fragility of this mechanism.

The figures highlight a central dimension of the Deaf Legal Illusion: while legal routes exist, they are structured in ways that make them largely inaccessible or ineffective for most deaf claimants.

VI. Conclusion

Across the instruments examined in this chapter, the pattern is clear: legal frameworks that appear to recognise and protect deaf people's rights often do so in ways that are partial, procedural, or impractical. That is the Deaf Legal Illusion. The ability of deaf people to challenge the inequalities they experience is severely restricted at various degrees with regard to the Human Rights Convention, the Disability Convention, and the EqA 2010.

The Human Rights Convention is generally accepted as a genuine system of law, albeit of a formal nature. There has been a number of Convention cases considering whether the human rights of deaf individuals have been infringed; however,

[138] GOV.UK, 'Civil Justice Statistics Quarterly: October to December 2024' (6 March 2025), www.gov.uk/government/statistics/civil-justice-statistics-quarterly-october-to-december-2024.
[139] ibid.

once again, the opportunity for deaf people to challenge oppression utilising the Human Rights Convention is severely limited due in part to the difficulty in bringing cases to the Court, but also to the fact that discrimination alone cannot be challenged unless one of the absolute rights has also been infringed.

The Disability Convention, in contrast, is both substantive and transformative, as it enshrines in international law for the first time sign language rights, and an obligation on state signatories to accept and facilitate sign language and more besides, fully recognising the dignity, equal worth and identify of deaf people. There is also evidence to suggest that the UK courts – the Supreme Court in this instance – are willing to consider the Disability Convention's provisions as part of its decision-making process. Once again, however, challenging oppression is confined to an individual enforcement model, and there has been little take-up of its individual complaint procedure to date, although initial results appear to be encouraging once the admissibility hurdle has been overcome. In addition, there is no legal obligation on states to respond to and address the views of the Committee on individual complaints, as in the case of *Lockrey* and *Beasley*.

On the whole, there is more scope available to challenge inequality within the EqA 2010, as deaf individuals can expect employers and service providers to implement adjustments. However, there is a clear divide with regard to the *nature* of the adjustments; that is, single, one-off adjustments with respect of a provision, criterion or practice or a physical feature are more likely to be considered reasonable than recurrent adjustments to address the lack of an auxiliary aid, which is the type of adjustment that deaf people will need, usually in the form of communication professionals such as BSL-English interpreters, lipspeakers or Palantypists.

The EqA 2010 is a game of two halves, as its PSED provisions are a strong example of transformative equality and go some way to 'cure' the 'disease' that is inequality by encouraging social inclusion by way of active measures to integrate marginalised groups in society. However, the lack of enforcement mechanism, relying only on the generally difficult route of judicial review or the EHRC's somewhat limited enforcement mechanisms, poses a barrier to deaf people who wish to challenge inequality through this route.

Taken together, these three instruments: the Human Rights Convention, the Disability Convention, and the EqA 2010, form the foundation of equality law in the UK. On paper, they promise protection, dignity, and recognition. But as this chapter has shown, their provisions often rely on narrow definitions, discretionary interpretations, or enforcement models that are inaccessible to many deaf people. That is the core of the Deaf Legal Illusion. Current equality law can only do so much at present, and it can only ever be a small part of the solution.[140]

[140] Colm O'Cinneide, 'Equality: Current and Future Directions of Travel' (The Equality Act 2010: five-years on conference, Chester, June 2015).

4

The Deaf Legal Dilemma

There is a legal bind at the heart of deaf people's experience with equality law: to gain protection, they must accept a legal identity that frequently misrepresents who they are. The issue is not that deaf people are never disabled. The problem lies in the requirement that all deaf people must be positioned within the legal category of disability in order to be seen, heard, and protected by law. Legal protection is not offered on deaf terms; it is extended through frameworks that define being deaf as a loss, an impairment, or a lack, which deny the cultural, linguistic, and community dimensions that many deaf people see as central to their identity.

This is the Deaf Legal Dilemma: a persistent and unresolved tension between legal recognition and cultural truth. Inclusion is offered, but on conditional terms. To be recognised, deaf people must misidentify themselves. They must speak in legal categories that flatten difference, erase language, and render deafhood invisible. And if they refuse – if they assert their identity as signers or as members of a linguistic and cultural minority – they will find themselves excluded from legal protections altogether.

The purpose of this chapter is to map the contours of this dilemma by examining how legal, policy, and rights-based frameworks attempt to define and categorise deaf people. It begins with an exploration of models of disability: medical, social, minority, cultural, and human rights, each of which offers partial recognition, but ultimately falls short of representing deaf lives on their own terms. The chapter then turns to alternative conceptualisations of deaf people as a language minority, as a culturo-lingusitic group, and as members of an ethnic or Indigenous group. These framings bring us closer to recognition, but even they are constrained by hearing-centric assumptions, legal formalism, and limited enforceability.

At its core, this chapter asks not whether deaf people deserve protection, but why that protection continues to require a distortion of identity. If the law cannot recognise deaf people without misnaming them, then the problem is not with deaf people but with the law itself.

I. Deaf People as Disabled? Models of Disability and their Limits

Deaf people reject the suggestion that they have an impairment or disability; deaf people are not ambivalent about being deaf, they think it is a fine thing to be deaf and favour more of it.[1] Lane argues that 'disowning the disability label would be the honest thing to do',[2] particularly as the provisions that society makes for disabled people often do not suit the interests of deaf people and may even run counter to them.[3] He concludes that the disability label deflects attention from the need for social reforms and encourages the technologists of normalisation in their eugenic and surgical programmes aimed at eliminating or severely reducing the ranks of culturally deaf people.[4] Nonetheless, some deaf people have embraced the label strategically, gaining access to rights through the Equality Act 2010 (EqA 2010), disability benefits, and employment support schemes. If they had not accepted the label – predominantly through the medical model – they would have no rights whatsoever, other than those afforded to hearing people.

The word 'normal' only entered the English language around 1840,[5] at a time when governments were classifying and controlling populations.[6] Disability presents itself to the so-called 'normal' observer through two modalities: function (inability to walk, hear, see); and appearance (a body marked by prosthesis, sign language, a wheelchair).[7] The gaze of the non-disabled both constructs and controls disability, provoking emotional responses such as fear, pity, or avoidance.[8] Davis elaborates that 'the average, well-meaning "normal" observer feels sorry for that disabled person, feels awkward about relating to them, believes that the government or charity should provide special services, and gives thanks for not being disabled'.[9] Deaf people too are caught in this system of normalisation because they lack a key sense: hearing.

Indeed, Woodward documents the existence of a widespread and powerful interpretation of deaf people as 'pathological' and 'fundamentally deficient'. This ideology has led to a focus on the facts of hearing impairment, and to classify deaf people in terms of the degree of their impairment. Other facts about them, such as their social and cultural lives, are then interpreted as consequences of these classifications.[10] This results in barriers when deaf individuals aspire to a full education and employment (see chapter one). According to Lane, this restriction of opportunity is socially constructed, not a direct result of being deaf.[11]

For abled people, disability is reduced to a visible marker, with writers such as Davis adopting a simplistic materialist view: 'almost by definition deaf persons . . .

[1] Harlan L Lane, 'Do Deaf People Have a Disability?' (2002) 2 *Sign Language Studies* 356, 369.
[2] ibid.
[3] ibid 369–70.
[4] ibid 370.
[5] Lennard J Davis, *Enforcing Normalcy: Disability, Deafness, and the Body* (Verso, 1995) 24.
[6] Michael Oliver and Colin Barnes, *The New Politics of Disablement* (Palgrave Macmillan, 2012) 19.
[7] ibid 11.
[8] ibid 12.
[9] Davis (n 5) 1–2.
[10] C Padden and T Humphries, *Deaf in America: Voices from a Culture* (Harvard University Press, 1990) 10.
[11] Lane (n 1) 364.

have a disability'.[12] Such framing leads to bad questions and worse answers.[13] Instead, this raises a deeper question: what is disability, and how is it constructed socially? Davis suggests disability is an absolute: 'one is either disabled or not'.[14] But he also argues that a disability is not an 'object' but a social role.[15] In that sense, normalcy and disability are co-produced, and one cannot exist without the other.[16]

Because able-bodiedness is the default, services do not name themselves. Public transport means transport for the able-bodied; it is only disabled people who need qualifiers: a wheelchair space, a disabled toilet.[17] But the object of disability discourse is not the disabled person, it is the social structures that define and manage the body. Disabled people are therefore engaged in a struggle over naming: the power to reject definitions that marginalise and to affirm those that dignify.[18] The language of resistance is often combative: a war, a battle, signalling the force that is required to shift entrenched norms. Barnes calls this institutional discrimination: so deeply embedded that its removal would cut across public and private systems alike. Confronting this requires political positioning.[19]

Finally, understandings of disability are not only lived but also embedded in legal and policy frameworks. For many, the global spread of human rights has been a pivotal political development.[20] When law protects disabled people, it tends to do so via civil rights, anti-discrimination law, or human rights mechanisms.[21]

Throughout disability discourse, two models are most commonly cited: the medical (or individual) model, and the social model. Knight explains that the medical model locates disadvantage in the individual's functional limitation, which must be treated or cured.[22] In contrast, the social model accepts that impairment exists but places responsibility for disadvantage on structural inequalities.[23] It is to these models that we now turn, alongside three others relevant to deaf people: the minority group model, the cultural model, and the human rights model.

[12] Thomas P Gonsoulin, 'Cochlear Implant/Deaf World Dispute: Different Bottom Elephants' 125 *Otolaryngology – Head and Neck Surgery* 552, 554.
[13] Lane (n 1) 296.
[14] Davis (n 5) x.
[15] ibid.
[16] ibid.
[17] Vic Finkelstein, 'Representing Disability' in John Swain and others (eds), *Disability Barriers – Enabling Environments* (SAGE Publications, 2004) 19.
[18] Len Barton, *Disability and Society: Emerging Issues and Insights* (Longman, 1996) 11.
[19] ibid 11–12.
[20] John Swain, 'International Perspectives on Disability' in John Swain and others (eds), *Disability Barriers – Enabling Environments* (SAGE Publications, 2004) 57.
[21] Rachel Hurst, 'Legislation and Human Rights' in John Swain and others (eds), *Disability Barriers – Enabling Environments* (SAGE Publications, 2004) 297.
[22] Pamela Knight, 'Deafness and Disability' in Susan Gregory and others (eds), *Issues in Deaf Education* (David Fulton Publishers, 1998) 215.
[23] Union of the Physically Impaired Against Segregation and Disability Alliance, 'Fundamental Principles of Disability' 3–4, https://disability-studies.leeds.ac.uk/wp-content/uploads/sites/40/library/UPIAS-fundamental-principles.pdf.

II. The Medical or Individual Model

Traditionally, disability has been understood as a medical condition or illness, and this framing influences how disability is defined and how legislation is interpreted.[24] The effect of this approach is that disabled persons must identify their medical condition and explain why they cannot participate in society in a 'normal' way.[25] This reinforces ideas of biological or physiological inferiority, contributes to a dependency model of disability, and may offer limited protection against disability discrimination simply because the focus is on conformity rather than the social environment.[26] Let us consider how this plays out in practice.

In the UK, disability is defined in EqA 2010, section 6(1) as a 'physical or mental impairment that has a substantial and long-term adverse effect on P's ability to carry out normal day-to-day activities'. McColgan confirms this definition reflects a medical rather than a social one.[27] Monaghan too confirms that one of the main criticisms about the definition is that it adopts a medical rather than social concept of disability[28] as it focuses on diagnosis and functional ability.[29]

Within the European Union, while the Employment Equality Directive[30] does not include a definition of disability or guidance on who is to be protected from discrimination on the grounds of disability, the European Court of Justice has defined disability as: 'a limitation which results in particular from physical, mental or psychological impairments and which hinder the participation of the person concerned in professional life'.[31] By framing disadvantage this way, the definition places the burden squarely at the disabled person's door.[32]

On the flip side of the coin, Waddington and Lawson argue that a medicalised definition is not always problematic in practice, as it serves the sole purpose of establishing that a disability exists in order to effect the law's protections.[33] Wells and Whittle concur that some reference to impairment is necessary to establish the threshold for legal protection.[34]

[24] Nicholas Bamforth, Maleiha Malik and Colm O'Cinneide, *Discrimination Law: Theory and Context, Text and Materials* (Sweet & Maxwell 2008) 977.

[25] ibid 977.

[26] Dagmar Schiek, Lisa Waddington and Mark Bell, *Cases, Materials and Text on National, Supranational and International Non-Discrimination Law* (Hart Publishing, 2007) 132.

[27] Aileen McColgan, *Discrimination Law: Text, Cases and Materials* (Hart Publishing, 2005) 566.

[28] Karon Monaghan, *Blackstone's Guide to the Disability Discrimination Legislation* (Oxford University Press, 2005) 18.

[29] ibid 64.

[30] Council Directive 2000/78/EC of 27 November 2000 establishing a general framework for equal treatment in employment and occupation.

[31] Case C-13/05 *Chacón Navas v Eurest Colectividades SA* 2006 ECR 1-6467.

[32] Lisa Waddington and Anna Lawson, 'Disability and Non-Discrimination Law in the European Union' (European Commission, 2009) 18, https://publications.europa.eu/en/publication-detail/-/publication/cf7bc8c8-2c84-46ff-83b5-202a6fb805a1.

[33] ibid 24.

[34] Katie Wells, 'The Impact of the Framework Employment Directive on UK Disability Discrimination Law' (2003) 32 *Industrial Law Journal* 253, 261; R Whittle, 'The Framework Directive for Equal Treatment in Employment and Occupation: An Analysis from a Disability Rights Perspective' (2002) 27 *European Law Review* 303, 324.

A. The Social Model

In contrast to the medical model of disability, Oliver argues that it is not the impairment that is the sole cause of problems in the lives of disabled people, but society itself, in terms of attitudes, infrastructure, building design and transport provision.[35] It was the Union of the Physically Impaired Against Segregation's (UPIAS) discussion paper, *Fundamental Principles of Disability*,[36] that turned the understanding of disability by arguing that it was not impairment that was the main cause of the social exclusion of disabled people but the way society responded to people with impairments.[37] This then led Oliver to coin the term, 'social model of disability'.[38]

There has been much discussion regarding the social model of disability as a theory, but Oliver insists that it is a practical tool, and that too much time has been spent discussing it rather than using it to drive change.[39] Its purpose is to expose and tackle institutional discrimination.[40] Oliver attributes the model's inspiration to the UPIAS, but Shakespeare argues that the social model was not, and has never been, the only social-contextual approach to understanding the disability experience, and points to earlier frameworks that predated Oliver's.[41]

Shakespeare argues that the social model was crucial to the British disability movement for two reasons. First, it identified a political strategy: barrier removal. If people with impairments are disabled by society, then the priority is to dismantle those barriers and promote the inclusion of people with impairments. In particular, if disability is the result of discrimination, then civil rights are the ultimate solution.[42] Second, the social model had a significant impact on disabled people themselves, as it enabled them to understand that it was society that was at fault, not themselves. They do not need to change; society needs to change.[43] The social model also encouraged academics to turn their attention to topics such as discrimination, the relationship between disability and industrial capitalism, and cultural representations of people with impairment.[44]

To place the social model of disability in dialogue with deaf experience, Corker explains that communication barriers arise not because deaf people cannot speak, but because society does not speak their language.[45] This reframing aligns with the

[35] Kingsley Purdam and others, 'Disability in the UK: Measuring Equality' (2008) 23 *Disability & Society* 53 65, 56.

[36] Union of the Physically Impaired Against Segregation and Disability Alliance (n 23).

[37] Michael Oliver, *Understanding Disability: From Theory to Practice*, 2nd edn (Palgrave Macmillan, 2009) 43.

[38] ibid.

[39] ibid 57.

[40] ibid 9.

[41] Tom Shakespeare, *Disability Rights and Wrongs* (Routledge, 2006) 13.

[42] ibid 30.

[43] ibid.

[44] ibid.

[45] Oliver (n 37) 57.

social model's core insight: that exclusion is produced by social arrangements, not individual deficit.

Oliver identifies five main criticisms of the social model that have come from within the disabled people's movement and disability studies. First, the social model ignores or is unable to deal adequately with the realities of impairment. Second, it overlooks the subjective experiences of 'pain' associated with both impairment and disability. Shakespeare argues that the social model needs to be reconceptualised to include the experience of impairment, and that this might be achieved by a more rigorous analysis of the role of culture in the oppression of disabled people.[46] He argues that there can be no impairment without society, nor disability without impairment: 'it is difficult to determine where impairment ends and disability starts'.[47] It is necessary to have an impairment in order to experience disabling barriers, and without this link, disability becomes a much broader, vaguer term which describes any form of socially imposed restriction. What counts as impairment is also a social judgement, as the meaning of impairment is a cultural issue, related to the values and attitudes of the wider society.[48]

Bamforth, Malik and O'Cinneide agree that the social model analysis can place too much emphasis upon externally imposed barriers and can overlook or neglect the reality of the functional limitations that may affect individuals.[49] In response to the separation of impairment and disability, Oliver makes it clear that it is not about the personal experience of impairment, but the collective experience of disablement.[50]

Third, the social model has been criticised for failing to incorporate other social divisions such as race, gender, ageing and sexuality. Oliver responds that while the model has not yet integrated these dimensions, that does not mean it cannot.[51] He goes as far as to say: '[it would be] far better if critics had spent less of their time criticising the social model for its perceived failures and instead put more effort into attempting to apply it in areas of racism, sexism and homosexuality'.[52] This is encouraging for Deaf Studies academics, as it suggests scope for integrating deaf discourse into the social model of disability.[53]

Fourth, critics argue that it is not only physical and environmental barriers that disable people, but also the cultural values that position them. Oliver counters that moving disability politics into the realm of representation is fundamentally misguided when so many still face material deprivation.[54] It has also been criticised for failing to offer a comprehensive theory of disablement. Oliver responds that

[46] Barton (n 18) 48.
[47] Shakespeare (n 41) 38.
[48] ibid 34–5.
[49] Bamforth, Malik and O'Cinneide (n 24) 978.
[50] Oliver (n 37) 48.
[51] ibid 49.
[52] ibid.
[53] Mairian Corker, *Deaf and Disabled, or Deafness Disabled? Towards a Human Rights Perspective* (Open University Press, 1998) 49.
[54] Oliver (n 37) 49.

it was never intended as such, and that theoretical development is still needed.[55] Shakespeare supports this, noting that the model has remained static for over 30 years, unlike other social movement ideologies such as feminism.[56] Expanding this point, Corker questions whether the social model is flexible enough to include the diversity of the deaf experience in a meaningful and acceptable way.[57] She suggests that deaf people have been excluded from the development of the social model.[58]

The European Court of Justice has interpreted disability under the Employment Equality Directive as a limitation resulting from impairment that hinders participation in professional life. This definition, set out in the case of *Chacón Navas*,[59] has generally been understood to reflect a medical model, since it places the burden on the individual. However, the reference to participation introduces a contextual element. While still predominantly medical, this aspect gestures toward a social model understanding, acknowledging that societal structures, the 'participation of the person concerned in professional life', contribute to disadvantage.

The influence of the social model is also evident in the Disability Convention. It defines persons with disabilities as those 'who have long-term physical, mental, intellectual or sensory impairments which in interaction with various barriers may hinder their full and effective participation in society on an equal basis with others'.[60] This language blends medical and social understandings of disability. Shakespeare refers to this as an 'interactional model',[61] which recognises that disability emerges through the dynamic between individual and structural factors.[62]

B. The Minority Group Model

An alternative to the social model is the socio-political or 'minority group' perspective on disability. According to this model, disability is the product of a constant interaction between the individual and their environment. Due to power dynamics in society, some groups are more disadvantaged than others, which means that more attention should be paid to anti-discrimination and equal opportunity measures rather than requiring disabled individuals to adapt to a non-disabled world.[63] Shakespeare explains that the notion of disabled people as a minority group is a North American approach, contrasted with the British social model which sought

[55] ibid.
[56] Shakespeare (n 41) 34.
[57] Corker (n 53) 6.
[58] ibid 38.
[59] *Chacón Navas v Eurest Colectividades SA* (n 31).
[60] United Nations, Convention on the Rights of Persons with Disabilities A/61/611 (2006), www.un.org/disabilities/documents/convention/convoptprot-e.pdf, Art 1.
[61] Shakespeare (n 41) 74–5.
[62] Paul Harpur and Heather Douglas, 'Disability and Domestic Violence: Protecting Survivors' Human Rights' (2015) 23 *Griffith Law Review* 405, 415.
[63] Aart Hendriks and Theresia Degener, 'The Evolution of a European Perspective on Disability Legislation' (1994) 1 *European Journal of Health Law* 343, 346–47.

to redefine disability as social oppression.[64] Essentially, the minority group model calls for civil rights legislation to guarantee individual rights to combat prejudice and discrimination against disabled people.[65]

The minority group model frames disability as a political and social status, not a personal tragedy or medical condition. Rooted in United States civil rights discourse, it draws parallels with race, gender, and ethnicity, arguing that disabled people are subject to systematic discrimination and institutional barriers. As Hahn explains, the model 'stresses attitudinal discrimination as the principal problem facing disabled persons' and calls for structural remedies, such as anti-discrimination legislation, rather than medical or charitable responses.[66]

A legal example of this model in practice is the Americans with Disabilities Act 1990, which adopts a minority rights approach. The statute states: 'Individuals with disabilities are a discrete and insular minority who have been faced with restrictions and limitations, subjected to a history of purposeful unequal treatment and relegated to a position of political powerlessness in our society.'[67] This is a clear example of how the minority group model treats disabled people as a group that has been sidelined, and argues that the law needs to step in and protect them in the same way it does with other marginalised groups.

However, applying the model is not straightforward. This approach has been criticised for encouraging an excessive emphasis upon defining who falls within the definition of 'disabled', which is a contentious issue that could limit the reach and effectiveness of disability discrimination legislation.[68] As Scotch explains, 'Exclusion and discriminatory treatment alone do not inherently generate collective identity or collective political action.'[69] This reflects a wider difficulty with applying traditional minority group definitions to disability, as Altman also observes, noting that disability is described as a 'complicated, multidimensional concept' that resists a single or fixed definition, especially one grounded in clear-cut group membership.[70]

Bamforth, Malik and O'Cinneide further argue that disabled persons often do not see themselves as part of a distinct social group and there is no real shared historical or social experience beyond a degree of shared disadvantage, which can vary considerably from group to group.[71] Killian agrees, referring to these shared experiences as 'cohesive social features', adding shared culture,

[64] Shakespeare (n 41) 24.

[65] ibid.

[66] Harlan Hahn, 'Antidiscrimination Laws and Social Research on Disability: The Minority Group Perspective' (1996) 14 *Behavioral Sciences & the Law* 41, 41.

[67] Americans with Disabilities Act 1990, s 2(a)(7).

[68] Bamforth, Malik and O'Cinneide (n 24) 980.

[69] Richard K Scotch, 'Disability as the Basis for a Social Movement: Advocacy and the Politics of Definition' (1988) 44 *Journal of Social Issues* 159, 160.

[70] Barbara M Altman, 'Definitions, Models, Classifications, Schemes, and Applications' in Gary Albrecht, Katherine Seelman and Michael Bury (eds), *Handbook of Disability Studies* (SAGE Publications, Inc, 2001) 97, https://sk.sagepub.com/reference/hdbk_disability.

[71] Bamforth, Malik and O'Cinneide (n 24) 981.

language, and geography.[72] Scotch makes a similar point, adding that discrimination alone does not automatically create group cohesion, and that there is no shared culture or language to anchor that identity. In many cases, disabled people do not identify themselves as part of a unified group, and the absence of a clear-cut boundary around 'disability' has long made it difficult to organise or legislate on this basis.

In addition, there is an argument that it could reinforce perceptions of the separateness of disabled groups from the mainstream of society, trigger competition for resources, and generate tensions within different disabled groups themselves as to who should come under the umbrella of 'disability'.[73] Degener has also cautioned that there is a need to avoid essentialism[74] – the assumption that all disabled people share the same fixed traits – and that disability is the defining feature of their identity rather than aspects shared by broader social and cultural contexts. This runs the risk of trapping disabled persons in similar stereotypes as those that have contributed to their social exclusion.[75]

When the minority group model is applied to deaf people, however, some of these criticisms begin to fall away. Deaf communities often do exhibit the cohesive features typically associated with minority groups: a shared language (sign languages), strong internal networks, and a positive sense of group identity. Unlike many disabled people who seek integration, many deaf people embrace separation. This gives the model more traction. And yet, even here, its focus on structural discrimination and civil rights may not go far enough. Deaf identity is not only about exclusion; it is about language, culture, and epistemology, dimensions the minority group model does not fully engage.

As noted earlier, the minority group model's approach to combating discrimination is to deal with institutional discrimination.[76] An example of how it might work in practice comes from Sweden. In the late 1990s a gang of deaf youths in Örebro carried out a number of violent acts against random hearing residents, claiming it was a response to years of oppression as a minority.[77] In response, the Örebro police department began training officers in Swedish Sign Language, and a range of initiatives were implemented to promote sign language and acknowledge previously neglected social problems.[78] This example shows how structural responses, rather than individual interventions, can address group-level disadvantage, aligning with the goals of the minority group model.

However, while this approach resonates strongly with deaf identity and political framing, it still leaves open questions about how best to capture the cultural

[72] Lewis M Killian, 'What or Who Is a "Minority"?' [1996] *Michigan Sociological Review* 18.

[73] Bamforth, Malik and O'Cinneide (n 24) 981.

[74] Theresia Degener, 'Disabled Persons and Human Rights: The Legal Framework' in Theresia Degener and Yolan Koster-Dreese (eds), *Human Rights and Disabled Persons* (Kluwer Academic, 1995) 9.

[75] ibid.

[76] Bamforth, Malik and O'Cinneide (n 24) 336.

[77] Ingrid Rindal Lundeberg and Jan-Kåre Breivik, 'Being Deaf in Court' (2015) 17 *Scandinavian Journal of Disability Research* 42, 44–45.

[78] ibid 46.

and linguistic dimensions of the deaf experience. What happens when the basis of group identity is not just discrimination, but shared collective features? Can a rights-based model built around exclusion really speak to communities built around belonging? And what gets missed when legal frameworks recognise disadvantage, but not the values the group wants protected? It is to these issues that the cultural model now turns.

C. The Cultural Model

Since the politicisation of disability by the international disabled people's movement, a growing number of academics have reconceptualised disability as a complex and sophisticated form of social oppression or institutional discrimination, comparable with sexism, homophobia and racism. This shift in analysis has moved attention away from individual impairments and toward the wider social and environmental factors that affect disabled individuals. However, it is argued that these studies have underexplored the role of culture, meaning a communally held set of values and beliefs, in the shaping of the oppression of disabled people.[79] Lawson argues that the emergence of the cultural model could be seen as a response to the dominance of the social model,[80] particularly its emphasis on structural barriers over lived, cultural experience.

In this way, the cultural model is emerging in response to the limitations of the medical, social, and minority group models. It differs in three ways: first, it emphasises the different ways disability is understood in varying cultural and social contexts, recognising disability as an existential, technical, and social phenomenon, in other words something defined and reflected by culture itself. Second, it reinterprets the social model's focus on lack of access or inaccessible or misrepresentative information, placing cultural representation at the centre of how disability is constructed and contested. Finally, it focuses on culturally rooted identities in which people develop, perform, and affirm a positive sense of disability, rather than seeking to overcome and reject it.[81]

This model, however, is not without criticism. Vernon points out that disabled people are not a homogeneous group, so any notion that 'disability culture' is universal for all disabled people needs to be challenged.[82] Concepts of culture amongst disabled people have varied dimensions, such as the feelings of disabled

[79] Barton (n 18) 48.

[80] John Lawson, 'Disability as a Cultural Identity' (2001) 11 *International Studies in Sociology of Education* 203, 215.

[81] Patrick J Devlieger, 'Generating a Cultural Model of Disability', 19th Congress of the European Federation of Associations of Teachers of the Deaf (2005) 8, www.researchgate.net/profile/Patrick_Devlieger/publication/237762101_Generating_a_cultural_model_of_disability/links/5434004f0cf2dc341daf2bc1.pdf.

[82] Ayesha Vernon, Colin Barnes, and Geoff Mercer, 'Reflexivity: The Dilemmas of Researching from the Inside', *Doing Disability Research* (The Disability Press, 1997).

people who also consider themselves to belong to other oppressed groups, for example; disabled women and, more specifically, Black disabled women.[83]

There is nonetheless a considerable body of work that clearly establishes the existence of a deaf culture, suggesting that this model of disability may be particularly effective in understanding the experiences of deaf people. It is able to accommodate the existence of a distinct language, community values, and epistemology. Rather than framing deafness as a lack or deficit, the cultural model can recognise it as a culturo-linguistic identity. This aligns with how many deaf people understand themselves and shifts the conversation away from access and accommodation toward recognition and respect.

D. The Human Rights Model

Emerging in part as a critique of the limitations of both the social and medical models, the human rights model of disability is grounded in the principles of dignity, equality, and participation. It is closely tied to the Disability Convention, which reflects this shift in international thinking. Degener explains that the human rights model moves beyond merely explaining disability (as the social model does) and instead anchors disability policy in human rights values, principally that the presence of impairment does not diminish a person's rights, dignity, or personhood.[84]

The human rights model holds that the 'problem' lies not in the individual's impairment, but in the way society is structured. However, unlike the social model, it explicitly frames this as a legal and moral issue. Human rights are seen as universal, and disability does not, and must not, exclude anyone from legal capacity or participation in society. As Degener and Quinn put it, 'The human rights model focuses on the inherent dignity of the human being and subsequently, but only if necessary, on the person's medical characteristics.'[85]

This model also explicitly incorporates both sets of rights: civil and political rights (such as legal capacity and freedom from violence) as well as economic, social, and cultural rights (such as health, education, and work).[86] In this sense, it is broader than the social model's usual focus on anti-discrimination law and barrier removal. Degener identifies six defining features of the human rights model. First, it affirms that impairment does not diminish a person's capacity to hold rights since rights do not depend on health status or bodily function. Second, the model encompasses the full spectrum of human rights, including both civil and political rights, and economic, social, and cultural rights.

[83] Lawson (n 80) 215.

[84] Theresia Degener, 'A New Human Rights Model of Disability' in Valentina Della Fina (ed), *The United Nations Convention on the Rights of Persons with Disabilities* (Springer, 2017).

[85] Gerard Quinn and others, 'Human Rights and Disability: The Current Use and Future Potential of United Nations Human Rights Instruments in the Context of Disability' (United Nations Press, 2002) 14.

[86] Theresia Degener, 'Disability in a Human Rights Context' (2016) 5 *Laws* 35, 38.

Third, it embraces impairment as a natural aspect of human diversity, to be respected rather than pathologised. Fourth, it acknowledges intersectionality by recognising that disability often interacts with other forms of inequality such as gender, race, and poverty. Fifth, while impairment prevention policies may have public health value, they must never compromise the dignity or rights of disabled people. Finally, the model positions itself as a roadmap for global justice, particularly by highlighting the structural exclusion of disabled people in the Global South and the need for transformative responses.[87] Taken together, these features closely align the model with the principle of transformative equality discussed in chapter two.

However, the human rights model also poses challenges. It assumes that states are willing and able to transform their legal and social systems, as discussed in chapter two. It also raises questions about enforcement, particularly where rights are recognised but remain unimplemented, as discussed in chapter three. Critics might argue that it still lacks clarity about how to reconcile universal human rights with the specific needs and epistemologies of marginalised groups, such as sign language communities, although this chapter seeks to address those tensions in relation to deaf people.

Nonetheless, for many the human rights model provides the clearest legal framework for realising deaf people's equality on their own terms, particularly when those terms include recognition of language, culture, and identity as integral to what justice means.

The medical, social, minority, cultural and human rights models of disability, as all models do, have their merits and their limitations. While this collective of disability models have served, and continue to serve, the needs of deaf people, they do not quite encapsulate the multifaceted dimensions of a deaf individual's identity, and instead focus only on their hearing status, or indeed, their disability status. The minority and cultural models show promise but are still tied up with the notion of disability, and consequently are unlikely to capture the cultural and language minority elements prevalent in deaf people.

III. Deaf People as a Language Minority

What if we understood deaf people not as disabled, but as a language minority? This framing shifts the emphasis from individual impairment to collective identity. There is a strong case for treating sign languages as minority languages, and while they are increasingly included in national language law, they are still often framed separately from spoken minority languages and not always afforded equivalent status or protection. Where such law does exist, it is often developed outside the framework of mainstream language legislation and tends to be shaped by disability or access policy rather than linguistic rights.

[87] ibid.

This framing matters. When deaf people are viewed through a language lens rather than a disability lens, it can lead to stronger cultural recognition, broader legal protections, and more favourable public perceptions. This chapter therefore considers how sign language law is positioned within broader legal frameworks. It begins by examining international and regional instruments, before turning to national legislation and concluding with a critical assessment of both.

A. International Legal Frameworks

International legal instruments reference language in various treaties, supporting Humphries and others' contention that a right to language can be implied.[88] Article 2 of the Universal Declaration of Human Rights[89] stipulates that everyone is entitled to all rights and freedoms enshrined in it, regardless of language.

At UN level, Article 27 of the International Covenant on Civil and Political Rights[90] confirms that recognised minorities have the right 'to use their own language'. Muhlke interprets Article 27 as meaning that a state may not prohibit the use of sign language among deaf people, nor make it impossible for them to meet each other, or pressure members of deaf communities to integrate into majority society.[91] In addition, scholars have argued that Article 27 obligates states to take positive steps to protect and promote linguistic minorities.[92] The Declaration on the Rights of Persons Belonging to National or Ethnic, Religious or Linguistic Minorities[93] expands on this, requiring states to provide opportunities for persons belonging to minorities to receive instruction in their mother tongue.[94] The UN Convention on the Rights of the Child similarly stipulates that children from linguistic minorities and Indigenous groups have the right to use their languages within their communities.[95]

In the European context, Article 14 of the Convention for the Protection of Human Rights and Fundamental Freedoms prohibits discrimination in the enjoyment of Convention rights on the grounds of language,[96] and Article 6(3)(a) affirms the right to understand legal proceedings,[97] including access to interpreters.[98] The

[88] Tom Humphries and others, 'The Right to Language' (2014) 41 *The Journal of Law, Medicine & Ethics* 872, 880.

[89] Universal Declaration of Human Rights 1948 (A/183/217)..

[90] United Nations, International Covenant on Civil and Political Rights 2200A (XXI) (1966).

[91] Anna-Miria Muhlke, 'The Right to Language and Linguistic Development: Deafness from a Human Rights Perspective' (2000) 40 *Virginia Journal of International Law* 705, 740.

[92] ibid.

[93] United Nations, Declaration on the Rights of Persons Belonging to National or Ethnic, Religious and Linguistic Minorities A/RES/47/135 (1992).

[94] Muhlke (n 91) 740.

[95] UNGA (20 November 1989) Convention on the Rights of the Child Resolution A/44/25, Art 30. United Nations, Convention on the Rights of the Child E/CN.4/RES/1990/74 Art 30.

[96] Convention for the Protection of Human Rights and Fundamental Freedoms 1950 (4XI1950).

[97] European Convention on Human Rights, Art 6(3)(a).

[98] Convention for the Protection of Human Rights and Fundamental Freedoms, Art 6(3)(e).

Council of Europe's European Charter for Regional and Minority Languages (ECRML) outlines more expansive protections, including the right to education in one's language, teaching of the language's history, and its use in courts, the media, cultural activities, and social and economic life.[99]

Despite longstanding calls for sign languages to be recognised under the ECRML, they remain excluded. While the Parliamentary Assembly and experts have repeatedly urged reform, including the establishment of a working group in 2019, no formal action has been taken. As argued elsewhere,[100] this inaction entrenches the perception that sign languages are not 'real' languages deserving of the same cultural and legal protections as spoken minority languages. This omission significantly limits the ECRML's utility for deaf communities in the UK and across Europe.

B. National Language Law

Dunbar argues for legislative intervention where speakers of minority languages face discrimination, particularly where language is closely tied to ethnicity or national origins.[101] McLeod adds that language legislation has become an essential strategy for sustaining minority languages, shaping institutional provision and enhancing language status. Legislation is now widely seen as a necessary tool in broader programmes of language revitalisation.[102]

While national language law typically refers to legislation protecting regional or minority spoken languages, sign language law is often framed differently. Historically associated with disability rights, sign languages have rarely been included in mainstream language legislation. Instead, dedicated sign language laws, such as the BSL (Scotland) Act 2015 or the Irish Sign Language Act 2017, have emerged to provide a legal framework for their use and promotion. These vary widely in scope, but all confer legal status on sign languages and form part of a state's national language law landscape.

Efforts by minority language communities to secure legislation for services, broadcasting, and education are motivated by a desire to participate in national life without sacrificing cultural and linguistic identity. Deaf people are no exception. Batterbury argues that formal sign language law gives deaf people actionable rights and clarifies the status of a national sign language as an

[99] Sarah CE Batterbury, 'Democratising Policy Theories: Enhancing Prospects for Language Justice for Sign Language Peoples' (2014) 42 *Policy & Politics* 547, 261.

[100] Rob Wilks and Filipe Venade De Sousa, 'Interpreting the European Charter for Regional and Minority Languages: Sign Languages as Regional and Minority Languages' (2025) 32 *The International Journal of Speech, Language and the Law* 62.

[101] Robert Dunbar, 'Language Legislation and Language Rights in the United Kingdom' (2002) 2 *European Yearbook of Minority Issues Online* 95, 185.

[102] Wilson McLeod, 'Securing the Status of Gaelic? Implementing the Gaelic Language (Scotland) Act 2005' [2006] *Scottish Affairs* 19, 20.

indigenous minority language.[103] It is seen as a route to equality that affirms deaf people's cultural and linguistic self-determination. While some laws are primarily symbolic, others can bring instrumental value: increasing the mobility of signers, supporting language acquisition in homes and schools, and improving access to services.

However, language policy in the UK is politically contested. Power struggles between dominant and subordinate language groups shape access to legal recognition and resources.[104] One only needs to compare the status of Welsh, Gaelic and BSL to see how variable legal outcomes can be. This approach comes with a warning from Krausneker: '[sign language law] will not solve all the problems of its users at once – and maybe not even in the near future'.[105]

C. Limitations of the Model

To assess whether sign language law achieves transformative equality, its limitations must be considered. De Meulder and Murray identify six common challenges. First, a disparity between deaf communities' expectations and the government's intentions during the drafting of the law. Second, constitutional recognition without implementing legislation, meaning legal effect is unlikely. Third, lack of funding, mechanisms or oversight to maintain rights, often resulting in inaction. Fourth, initial funding shortfalls. Fifth, limited long-term resource commitment. And sixth, challenges in constituting and maintaining sign language bodies.[106]

A medical or disability lens has led to confusion about the meaning of linguistic rights and has contributed to different treatment of sign languages compared to spoken ones.[107] BSL signers are the only group whose first language is not English who must rely on disability discrimination legislation to secure access to services in their own language. This is linked to deaf people's dual category status as both a linguistic minority and a disabled group,[108] and to the deficit framing discussed earlier in this chapter and in chapter one.[109] De Meulder and Murray argue that this has contributed to 'misunderstandings, myths and devaluating ideologies about sign languages' that are used, consciously or not, to deny legal status to sign languages.[110]

[103] Batterbury (n 99) 566.

[104] ibid 559.

[105] Verena Krausneker, 'Has Something Changed? Sign Languages in Europe: The Case of Minorised Minority Languages' (2003) 19 *Deaf Worlds: International Journal of Deaf Studies* 33, 11.

[106] Maartje De Meulder and Joseph J Murray, 'Buttering Their Bread on Both Sides?' (2017) 41 *Language Problems and Language Planning* 136–141, 144.

[107] ibid 136.

[108] Maartje De Meulder, 'The Influence of Deaf People's Dual Category Status on Sign Language Planning: The British Sign Language (Scotland) Act (2015)' (2017) 18 *Current Issues in Language Planning* 215, 215.

[109] De Meulder and Murray (n 106).

[110] ibid 143.

These framings influence how sign languages are discussed and legislated. For example, the Council of Europe's Resolution 2247 refers to sign languages as a 'means of communication' and a 'vehicle for ensuring inclusion', a framing not applied to spoken minority languages. Likewise, the BSL (Scotland) Act 2015 suggests that public authorities consult with 'persons who represent users of BSL', a formulation not seen in spoken language law. Such provisions reinforce deficit framings and obscure recognition of deaf people as a language minority.

Most sign language laws focus on interpreter provision, rather than promoting wider use of sign language in society. De Meulder argues that this reflects the primacy of the disability model: access becomes synonymous with interpretation.[111] This contrasts sharply with Gaelic language rights. Gaelic speakers have the right to access services from Gaelic-speaking staff, not via interpreters.[112] Sign language law also risks reinforcing the framing of sign languages as an 'accessible format' rather than as a language. Again, in Scotland, although national and local plans have been published, government reporting has been vague, data-light, and slow to address persistent gaps.[113] Similarly, UK government reports for the BSL Act 2022 show inconsistent departmental engagement, a focus on media-friendly announcements, and continued reliance on the EqA 2010 to frame BSL provision as a disability-related obligation.[114]

Political participation is hindered when legal recognition is not matched by resources, institutional reform, or inclusion. For example, following the enactment of the BSL (Scotland) Act 2015, members of the Scottish deaf community expressed uncertainty about how to engage with public consultations. Responses often revert to historical grievances rather than efforts to shape institutional practices.[115] This reflects Bryan and Emery's concern that law, while conferring rights, can also be used to prescribe the terms of deaf people's engagement with society.[116] However, De Meulder argues that the BSL (Scotland) Act 2015 nonetheless opened up space for new forms of dialogue between deaf signers and Scottish public authorities.[117]

The language minority model has potential to be the defining model capable of capturing the essence of the deaf identity that focuses on sign languages. However, not all deaf individuals have embraced sign languages, so what to do with those? Would a hybrid model work perhaps, a sort of 'disabled-language' model?

[111] Martje De Meulder, Joseph J Murray and Rachel L McKee, 'Introduction: The Legal Recognition of Sign Languages: Advocacy and Outcomes Around the World' in Martje De Meulder, Joseph J Murray and Rachel L McKee (eds), *The Legal Recognition of Sign Languages: Advocacy and Outcomes Around the World* (Multilingual Matters Ltd, 2019) 4.

[112] De Meulder and Murray (n 109) 142.

[113] Rob Wilks, 'From Barking Dogs to Roarless Dragons: The Legal Recognition of Sign Languages across the United Kingdom' (2026) 26 *Sign Language Studies*.

[114] ibid 15–18.

[115] Gordon Hay, Rachel O'Neill, and Rob Wilks, 'Scotland, BSL, Language Recognition and the Law' (Deaf Studies Conference, University of Wolverhampton, February 2019).

[116] De Meulder (n 108) 229.

[117] ibid.

IV. Beyond Minority

A. A Culturo linguistic Group

Ladd argues that deaf communities were swept along with the disability social model movement largely because it lacked the political power to articulate its own perspective. Despite efforts to include deaf people within its framework, the social model nonetheless reduces their experience to physical deafness, with a medical underpinning, such as access to flashing light doorbells, text telephones and subtitles.[118] As we have seen, it fails to account for the collective cultural and linguistic identity of deaf people.

Ladd introduces for a new perspective on deaf identity that he describes as the culturo-linguistic model. Rather than seeing deaf communities as disabled groups, or as a language minority, Deaf people are a distinct group to be understood on their own terms.[119] What distinguishes deaf communities as a distinct group is what Ladd terms deafhood,[120] and the use of a sign language shapes both cultural frameworks and worldviews in ways fundamentally different from other disability experiences.[121]

The term 'culturo' refers to a collective deaf identity shaped by visual experience, social norms, historical continuity, and resistance to audist oppression. Deaf culture is understood not as a set of customs or folklore, but as an epistemological framework transmitted through sign language and community spaces. It is also political. A cultural vacuum exists between a deaf person and the dominant society in terms of access to the information and culture of that society, and it is within that vacuum that deaf people experience their collective similarities and shape their collective responses.[122] Ladd also argues that culture consists of the stories we tell ourselves about ourselves, our place in the world, and the attitudes and behaviours we should adopt,[123] and there is evidence to suggest that deaf stories and folklore exist.[124]

The roots of deaf culture as a culturo-linguistic group are found in what Ladd calls 'deaf cultural sites',[125] such as residential schools and deaf clubs. Deaf schools have historically served as spaces for language acquisition, cultural socialisation, and preparation for life in a predominantly hearing society, often led by deaf adults.[126] Deaf clubs, many founded in the nineteenth century, have functioned as intergenerational spaces where sign languages are preserved, developed, and

[118] Paddy Ladd, *Understanding Deaf Culture: In Search of Deafhood* (Multilingual Matters, 2003) 15.
[119] ibid 15–17.
[120] A process by which deaf individuals come to actualise their deaf identity, ibid xviii.
[121] Wayne Morris, *Theology without Words: Theology in the Deaf Community* (Routledge, 2009) 13.
[122] Ladd (n 118) 254.
[123] ibid 255–56.
[124] Rachel Sutton-Spence and Michiko Kaneko, *Introducing Sign Language Literature: Folklore and Creativity* (Red Globe Press, 2016).
[125] Ladd (n 118) 297.
[126] ibid.

passed down.[127] They provide linguistic capital and sociocultural grounding, even as their physical presence declines in favour of more fluid online deaf spaces.[128] Ladd also points to deaf sport, visual and performing arts, communication media, working lives and higher education as vital aspects of deaf cultural life.[129]

The 'linguistic' dimension positions sign language as central: not merely as a tool for communication but as the foundation of deaf ways of being, knowing, and interacting with the world, whereby 'home' is the deaf community.[130] Ladd emphasises that sign languages are not only modes of communication, but the medium through which deaf culture is constructed and transmitted.[131] For deaf people, language is inseparable from identity: it determines not just how one communicates, but how one belongs. In this sense, the linguistic dimension of the culturo-linguistic model is as much about language socialisation and group membership as it is about functional access.

Yet the transmission of sign language is deeply uneven. Because over 90 per cent of deaf children are born to hearing parents, and sign language is rarely learned in the home, it cannot rely on the traditional intergenerational transmission found in spoken language communities.[132] Instead, language acquisition must be institutionally enabled, typically through deaf schools, community networks, or targeted early support. When these are absent or underfunded, as they often are, deaf children face language deprivation, a phenomenon that delays or impairs cognitive development, education, and social integration.[133]

Campaigns such as the British Deaf Association's *BSL in Our Hands*[134] highlight how fragmented and inaccessible current provision remains. Families often struggle to access BSL tuition, and even when services exist, they are inconsistently delivered. Sign language development is frequently treated as secondary to spoken language acquisition, a prioritisation that reflects ongoing tensions between disability and language minority framings. The culturo-linguistic model resists this dichotomy by insisting that sign language is not an optional extra, but a defining feature of deaf cultural life. Without access to sign language, deaf culture cannot be sustained.

The 'culturo-linguistic' model has found traction wider afield, specific in relation to culturo-linguistically congruent surroundings for people in care homes. Within this context, a culturo-linguistic environment is one where 'residents

[127] ibid 46.

[128] Gill Valentine and Tracey Skelton, 'Changing Spaces: The Role of the Internet in Shaping Deaf Geographies' (2008) 9 *Social & Cultural Geography* 469; Dai O'Brien, Lisa Stead and Nicholas Nourse, 'Bristol Deaf Memories: Archives, Nostalgia and the Loss of Community Space in the Deaf Community in Bristol' (2019) 20 *Social & Cultural Geography* 899.

[129] Ladd (n 118) 47–56.

[130] ibid 16.

[131] ibid 18.

[132] British Deaf Association, 'Position Statement on the Language Acquisition of Deaf Children' (2023), https://bda.org.uk/wp-content/uploads/2024/03/BDA-Early-Years-Position-Full-v1.docx.

[133] Lucy Wox, 'The Dignicide of Deaf Children: Is Language Deprivation a Breach of Their Human Rights?' (University of the West of England Bristol, in progress).

[134] British Deaf Association, 'BSL in Our Hands' (2025), https://bda.org.uk/bsl-in-our-hands.

reside with and are also cared for by people who can speak their language, understand their values, and which includes culturally appropriate facilities, activities and media access'.[135] This is quite helpful for our understanding of the culturo-linguistic model, as equality for deaf people would look exactly like that: a society and legal system that takes into account sign language, understands deaf values, and provides culturally appropriate facilities, activities, and media access.

One criticism of the culturo-linguistic model is that it does not clearly account for how deaf individuals raised in hearing families come to belong to deaf culture. In response, Ladd suggests that even when brought up outside deaf communities or in oral schools, there is a major impulse in mainstreamed deaf adolescents to pursue a journey towards deaf communities, towards redefining and reshaping one's self by moving from a hearing-impaired identity towards a deaf one.[136] He also argues that there is a high rate of endogamous marriage, with 90 per cent of all deaf people who marry marrying another deaf person:[137] 'Deaf people have one of the highest intermarriage rates of all social groupings.'[138] Thus, even though some deaf children born into hearing families may not necessarily be part of deaf culture throughout their childhood, unless they attend a deaf residential school or deaf clubs, they are statistically more likely to seek and enter the deaf community one way or another, thus becoming part of deaf culture in this way.

This model reframes deaf identity not through deficit but through shared language, culture, and experience. It challenges systems that treat sign language as compensatory, rather than constitutive. While not without its limitations, the culturo-linguistic model offers a lens that recognises deaf communities as intentional, resilient, and self-defining, shaped by collective history and sustained through deliberate cultural transmission.

B. An Ethnic Group

Another model of particular use is that of deaf ethnicity, developed by Lane, Pillard and Hedberg,[139] and expanded by Ladd and Lane.[140] They argue that if deafhood is the 'the sum of all meanings of what "deaf" might be', then deaf ethnicity is 'the collective manifestation of deafhoods', comprising 'collective language, identity, culture, history, arts, epistemologies and ontologies'.[141] Corker similarly suggests

[135] Conor Martin, 'Culturo-Linguistic Congruity in the Residential Care of the Elderly and Cognitively Impaired in North Wales' (MRes Dissertation, Bangor University, 2021) 93.

[136] Ladd (n 118) 258.

[137] ibid 254.

[138] ibid 386.

[139] Harlan L Lane, Richard C Pillard, and Ulf Hedberg, *People of the Eye: Deaf Ethnicity and Ancestry* (Oxford University Press, 2010).

[140] Paddy Ladd and Harlan L Lane, 'Deaf Ethnicity, Deafhood, and Their Relationship' (2013) 13 *Sign Language Studies* 565, 579.

[141] ibid 575–76.

that deaf people could fall under the legal category of 'race' enabling their cultural identity to be protected alongside their experience of oppression.[142]

An ethnic group is commonly defined as a community that shares a sense of ancestry, cultural tradition, and collective identity, and is recognised as such by both insiders and outsiders. Gordon describes it as a group that perceives itself to have historical ancestry and identity: a sense of peoplehood.[143] Schermerhorn similarly emphasises shared ancestry, memory, and symbolic cultural traits that define its collective distinctiveness.[144] Ladd and Lane identify a range of ethnic properties, including sign languages, bonding through community participation and endogamy, social institutions such as deaf schools and clubs, cultural production, boundary maintenance, and intergenerational socialisation.[145] They add that 'there is deaf ethnicity to be found wherever a sign language is found'.[146]

Section 9(1) EqA 2010 states that race includes 'colour, nationality, and ethnic or national origin'. There is no official definition of race, with the House of Lords in *Mandla v Dowell Lee* (*Mandla*)[147] referring to Simon LJ in *Ealing London Borough Council v Race Relations Board*[148] who stated that '"racial" is not a term of art, either legal . . . or scientific. I apprehend that anthropologists would dispute how far the word "race" is biologically at all relevant to the species amusingly called homo sapiens'.[149] This tells us how not to define race, and thus the definition of race should be used in its popular sense with a purposive approach. In *Mandla*, ethnic origin was defined as a cultural, rather than a strict racial question.[150] It was further held in *Chandhok and another v Tirkey*[151] that ethnic origin in section 9(1)(c) EqA 2010 had a wide and flexible ambit, suggesting that it would be, in theory, possible to widen the concept to include deaf ethnicity. So far, there does not appear to be any element of the attempts to define race that could preclude deaf people.

Returning to *Mandla*, Lord Fraser provided two essential characteristics: (1) a long-shared history, of which the group is conscious as distinguishing it from other groups, and the memory of which it keeps alive; and (2) a cultural tradition of its own, including family and social customs and manners. He further provided five relevant characteristics: (1) either a common geographical origin, or descent from a small number of common ancestors; (2) a common language, not necessarily peculiar to the group; (3) a common literature particular to the group; (4) a common religion different from that of neighbouring groups or from the general community surrounding it; and/or (5) being a minority or being an oppressed or

[142] Corker (n 53) 48.
[143] M Gordon, *The Scope of Sociology* (Oxford University Press, 1988) 129.
[144] Richard Alonzo Schermerhorn, *Comparative Ethnic Relations: A Framework for Theory and Research* (University of Chicago Press, 1978) 12.
[145] Ladd and Lane (n 140) 566.
[146] ibid 568.
[147] *Mandla and another v Dowell Lee and another* [1983] 2 AC 548.
[148] *Ealing London Borough Council v Race Relations Board* [1972] AC 342 [362].
[149] *Mandla v Dowell Lee* (n 147) [561].
[150] ibid 550.
[151] *Chandhok and another v Tirkey* UKEAT/0190/14/KN.

dominant group within a larger community.[152] It is not specified what weighting the words 'essential' and 'relevant' are given, so I assume that the two essential characteristics are mandatory requirements, and the relevant characteristics, where found, provide further evidence to support claims that particular groups are to be considered ethnic groups.

When applied to deaf communities, deaf people have the two essential characteristics: a long-shared history of which the group is conscious as distinguishing it from other groups, and the memory of which it keeps alive; and a cultural tradition, including family and social customs and manners.

Of the five relevant characteristics, there is evidence of four, the most obvious of which is the common language of BSL, common geographical origins whereby deaf people tend to congregate around the cities and towns where deaf schools and colleges are or have been prevalent, a common literature – both in written and BSL form – and a minority group that is arguably oppressed. In relation to geography, Ladd confirms that deaf communities do not generally choose to live in proximity, but that this is also true for other groups such as Jewish-Americans, and other former immigrant communities who initially lived together, which have subsequently dispersed, yet continue to claim a common cultural identity.[153]

In respect of the fifth relevant characteristic, there is very little in the way of academic research regarding the role that religion plays within the deaf community. One would be forgiven for assuming that this would not be a characteristic of the deaf community, given that most deaf people would have been born into a family who subscribe (if at all) to a particular religion. For example, if a deaf child was born into a white, Welsh family whose faith was that of the Church in Wales – that is, Anglican[154] – it is likely that that deaf child would be brought up by their parents to respect the doctrines of the Church in Wales. If that deaf child were then to discover their deaf identity and become involved with the deaf community, it is unlikely that their religion would change. The same would be true for a deaf child born into a Muslim, Sikh, Hindu or Jewish family.

However, Broesterhuizen argues that deaf people often have been outsiders in a hearing church, and that the message of the church has not reached deaf people because the language, symbols, culture of the traditional church, and the view of church people on deafness are remote from the culture and daily life experiences of deaf people.[155] Thus, it is arguable that the shape a 'deaf religion' could be in the form of union or collectivism whereby members of the deaf community may congregate according to their religion to practise their faith in their own language with their peers.

This argument is supported by the initial findings of the Scripture, Dissent and Deaf Space research project, which looked at the spaces produced for deaf people

[152] *Mandla v Dowell Lee* (n 147) [562].

[153] Ladd (n 118) 255.

[154] Church in Wales, 'Volume I: Prefatory Note' (2025), www.churchinwales.org.uk/en/clergy-and-members/constitution/volume-i-prefatory-note.

[155] Marcel Broesterhuizen, 'Faith in Deaf Culture' (2005) 66 *Theological Studies* 304, 304.

by the nineteenth-century Church of England by deaf people within the structure of those church spaces.[156] Gulliver confirms that the practice of religion by deaf people was more about having a core set of beliefs than a 'religion' per se, and that the core set was about validity as a visual people, which was manifested in choices around worship services in terms of visuality and language rather than what religion or denomination to follow.[157] It is thus argued that this separation could constitute 'deaf religion', not in terms of the faith itself, but in terms of how faith is practised. Indeed, there are BSL resources available for religions such as Christianity,[158] Judaism,[159] and Jehovah's Witnesses.[160]

Despite this, the ethnic model attracts criticism. Davis warns that framing deaf identity through ethnicity risks echoing the 'brutal history of racial politics', and may promote exclusion or essentialism.[161] He also argues that digital culture, mainstreaming, and the decline of deaf schools and clubs have weakened the collective 'otherness' that underpins deaf identity.[162]

Other criticisms include Sabatello's contention that there is a need to differentiate between those who are legally recognised as ethnic, linguistic and religious communities and 'other sorts of life-style cleavages, social movements and voluntary associations', and he clearly thinks that the deaf community is one of the latter.[163] Similarly, Tucker argues that rather than affording the deaf community ethnic status, they should embrace the wealth of opportunities and potential life experiences available to them with cochlear implants, rather than insist on being segregated from hearing people.[164] To counteract, Eckert argues that these two academics express major misunderstandings of deaf identity and culture,[165] and thus their views can be disregarded.

In conclusion, the ethnic model may not apply to all deaf individuals, but it does capture key features of cultural deaf communities in the UK and beyond. Recognising deaf people as an ethnic group under the EqA 2010 would offer a pathway to legal protection grounded in shared cultural identity, not individual impairment. As such, it remains a viable response to the Deaf Legal Dilemma.

[156] More information can be found at https://sdds.blogs.bristol.ac.uk.

[157] Mike Gulliver, 'Practice of Religion by Deaf People' (personal correspondence with the author, 14 May 2018).

[158] Christian BSL, 'Vocabulary, Prayers, Reflections, and Bible Passages in British Sign Language' (2025), https://christianbsl.com.

[159] Jewish Deaf Association, *Sign Language in Judaism* (2003).

[160] www.jw.org/bfi.

[161] Lennard J Davis, 'Deafness and the Riddle of Identity' (*The Chronicle*, 12 January 2007), www.lennarddavis.com/downloads/deafnessandtheriddle.pdf.

[162] ibid.

[163] M Sabatello, 'Disability, Cultural Minorities, and International Law: Reconsidering the Case of the Deaf Community' (2005) 26 *Whittier Law Review* 1025.

[164] Richard Clark Eckert, 'Toward a Theory of Deaf Ethnos: Deafnicity ≈ D/Deaf (Homaemon – Homoglosson – Homothreskon)' (2010) 15 *Journal of Deaf Studies and Deaf Education* 317, 319.

[165] ibid.

C. An Indigenous Group

What distinguishes Indigenous peoples from other 'minority groups' is their connection to traditional homelands, historical continuity, unique cultural practices, and a position of non-dominance.[166] An Indigenous group is generally understood as a community with historical continuity, cultural distinctiveness, and a sustained connection to a particular territory. This understanding is especially salient in contexts marked by colonisation, displacement, or marginalisation. While no single legal definition exists, Martínez Cobo identifies key features including self-identification,[167] membership of a community,[168] and the historical continuation of distinct cultural, political, and social systems.[169] Kingsbury considers Martínez Cobo's features to be part of an indicative rather than fixed definition, to be used flexibly in international law.[170]

The International Labour Organization's Indigenous and Tribal Peoples Convention ('the ILO Convention') describes Indigenous peoples as those who retain distinct institutions and identities regardless of their formal legal status.[171] A territorial element is also usually implied: the World Bank Policy on Indigenous Peoples suggests that having 'a close attachment to ancestral territories and to the natural resources in these areas'[172] is a key feature of indigeneity. Some definitions interpret 'place' symbolically or culturally, referring to the relationship between Indigenous groups and their environment as a source of life,[173] what is sometimes called the 'Indigenous place'.[174] Colonialism is also a recurring theme. The ILO Convention defines Indigenous peoples as those descended from populations inhabiting a country 'at the time of conquest or colonisation'.[175] Martínez Cobo similarly grounds his definition in historical continuity with pre-invasion and pre-colonial societies.[176]

[166] Jeff J Corntassel and Tomas Hopkins Primeau, 'The Paradox of Indigenous Identity: A Levels-of-Analysis Approach' (1998) 4 *Global Governance: A Review of Multilateralism and International Organizations* 139, 155.

[167] José R Martínez Cobo, 'Study of the Problem of Discrimination Against Indigenous Populations' (United Nations, 1986) E/CN.4/Sub.2/1986/7/Add.4, para 381.

[168] ibid para 380.

[169] ibid para 379.

[170] Benedict Kingsbury, 'Self-Determination and "Indigenous Peoples"' (1992) 86 *American Society of International Law Proceedings* 383, 385–86.

[171] International Labour Organization, 'Indigenous and Tribal Peoples Convention' (1989) No 169, Art 1(1)(b), https://normlex.ilo.org/dyn/nrmlx_en/f?p=NORMLEXPUB:12100:0::NO::P12100_ILO_CODE:C169.

[172] S Satish, 'The World Bank Policy on Indigenous Peoples' (South Asia Sector Social Development, 1999), https://documents1.worldbank.org/curated/en/535811468771538686/pdf/30438.pdf.

[173] Kirstin Hastrup and Karen Fog Olwig (eds), *Siting Culture: The Shifting Anthropological Object* (Routledge, 1997) 12.

[174] Andrea Muehlebach, '"Making Place" at the United Nations: Indigenous Cultural Politics at the U.N. Working Group on Indigenous Populations' (2001) 16 *Cultural Anthropology* 415, 416.

[175] International Labour Organization (n 171) Art 1(1)(a).

[176] Martínez Cobo (n 167) 379.

Deaf communities exhibit many of these features. As established elsewhere in this chapter, deaf people consistently identify as culturally distinct, bound by shared norms, values, and language, often transmitted intergenerationally outside of kinship structures. Their non-dominant status within hearing-majority societies, coupled with systemic barriers to participation, mirrors the marginalisation faced by other minority and Indigenous groups.[177] While deaf communities may not claim ancestral land or territories, they have historically coalesced around deaf cultural sites, often referred to as 'deaf spaces',[178] such as St John's Deaf Community Centre in Green Lanes, London.[179] Escobar refers to such spaces as a 'fundamental and multidimensional space for the creation and recreation of the ecological, economic, and cultural practices of communities'.[180]

Nonetheless, on the issue of ancestral land or territories, Woll and Ladd suggest that sign language-using deaf people have gathered together for at least 7,000 years, and that evidence of sign communication in various First Nations indicates that a deaf presence may be even older.[181] Existing research suggests that pockets of deaf communities existed and continue to exist around the world. A well-known, now ceased, example is that of Martha's Vineyard, an island off the East Coast of the United States, but there remain island communities in Providence Island near Columbia, Grand Cayman Island in the Caribbean, and Amami Island near Japan. There are also villages like Bengkala (Desa Kolok) in Bali, Adamorobe in Ghana, Nohya (Yucatec Mayas) in Mexico, Ban Khor in Thailand, Kosindo in Surinam, and Saint Elizabeth in Jamaica, and social groups like the Al-Sayyid Bedouins in Israel, the Urubu tribe in Brazil, and the Enga of Papua New Guinea.[182] Could these individual deaf communities, at the very least, be considered Indigenous groups?

Like many Indigenous peoples, deaf communities also resist assimilation into dominant norms. Patrick notes that 'culturally and linguistically distinct forms of education . . . have been threatened by states',[183] and that Indigenous peoples often seek to maintain collective identity through language and educational self-determination. In similar fashion, deaf movements have pursued deaf schools

[177] Ladd (n 118).

[178] Mike Gulliver, 'Places of Silence' in Frank Vanclay, Matthew Higgins and Adam Blackshaw (eds), *Making Sense of Place* (National Museum of Australia Press, 2008) 92.

[179] St John's Deaf Community Centre, 'About' (2023), https://sites.google.com/sjdcc.org.uk/stjohnsdeafcommunitycentre/noticeboards/About; William John Lyons, 'The Story of John P. Gloyn and "The City Road Congregation" (1872-1877), or How a Deaf-Led Deaf Space Came into Existence in Victorian North London' (2024) 21 *Cultural and Social History* 41.

[180] Arturo Escobar, 'Whose Knowledge, Whose Nature? Biodiversity, Conservation, and the Political Ecology of Social Movements' (1998) 5 *Journal of Political Ecology* 53, 69.

[181] Paddy Ladd and Bencie Woll, 'Deaf Communities' in Marc Marschark and Patricia Elizabeth Spencer (eds), *The Oxford Handbook of Deaf Studies, Language, and Education*, vol 1, 2nd edn (Oxford University Press, 2011).

[182] Annelies Kusters, 'Deaf Utopias? Reviewing the Sociocultural Literature on the World's "Martha's Vineyard Situations"' (2010) 15 *Journal of Deaf Studies and Deaf Education* 3, 3.

[183] Donna Patrick, 'Indigenous Contexts' in Marilyn Martin-Jones, Adrian Blackledge and Angela Creese (eds), *The Routledge Handbook of Multilingualism* (Routledge, 2012) 30.

rather than education in mainstream settings. On the matter of colonisation, I have explored this elsewhere in relation to deaf communities, concluding that deaf cultures are not only directly affected by majority cultures, but are also shaped by both acquiescence to and resistance against that cultural domination, marginalising Indigenous sign languages and cultural practices, and shaping contemporary discourse on deaf identity and legal systems.[184]

Still, there are clear limitations to framing deaf communities as Indigenous. While self-identification is central to international frameworks, there is no widespread movement within deaf communities to claim Indigenous status. Most definitions presume a relationship to land or ancestral territory, a condition deaf communities cannot fulfil in the conventional sense as, while 'deaf spaces' provide symbolic and social anchoring, they lack the geographic permanence typically required for Indigenous claims. Corntassel also cautions that extending Indigenous status to groups such as deaf people may blur legal boundaries and undermine Indigenous efforts at recognition based on colonisation and dispossession.[185]

Nevertheless, the Indigenous model is conceptually useful. It exposes the limits of legal frameworks that treat deaf people as disabled individuals requiring adjustment, rather than as members of a historically marginalised cultural group. It also aligns with broader claims for language rights, cultural integrity, and group-based autonomy. While unlikely to provide doctrinal recognition in international law, it helps situate deaf communities within a global discourse of cultural survivance and may strengthen arguments for collective legal status in national frameworks. As such, it contributes another dimension to the broader case being made throughout this chapter: that deaf people require structural, not individual, legal recognition.

V. The Deaf Rights Model

This chapter has explored the limits of equality law in recognising deaf people as they are. At the heart of the Deaf Legal Dilemma is a structural mismatch: legal protection is offered only when deaf people conform to the identity of 'disabled individuals', an identity that distorts their own cultural and linguistic self-understanding. The law claims to offer inclusion, but does so on terms that flatten difference, suppress self-definition, and reinforce hearing norms. What results is not meaningful recognition but legal misrepresentation.

To unpick this dilemma, the chapter examined how equality law situates deaf people exclusively within the category of disability. The law does not recognise deafness as a linguistic, cultural, or collective identity; only as a disability.

[184] Rob Wilks, 'Deaf Legal Theory: Challenging the Law's Hearing Bias' (2025) 30 *Journal of Deaf Studies and Deaf Education* 293, 299.
[185] Corntassel and Primeau (n 166) 151.

This legal framing is not neutral. It is rooted in the medical model, reinforced by elements of the social model, and only partially mitigated by human rights approaches that remain embedded in disability discourse. While these frameworks differ in emphasis, they converge in one crucial respect: they construct deaf people as subjects who must be managed, accommodated, or assisted, rather than as members of a language minority or a culturo-linguistic group whose identity falls outside the logic of impairment. The chapter contrasted this with a range of alternative models, particularly ethnic, and Indigenous, which, although not recognised in law, offer more accurate accounts of deaf people's lived realities.

In response, the chapter explored a set of alternative framings that more closely align with deaf people's lived experience: as a language minority, a culturo-linguistic group, an ethnic group, and potentially even as Indigenous. These models are not without risk: they carry definitional tensions, legal ambiguities, and potential for political resistance, yet they also offer a way out of the deficit-based logic that dominates current legal frameworks. Most importantly, they start from deaf people's own ways of knowing, organising, and identifying. They reverse the gaze: the question becomes not how deaf people fit into existing categories, but how those categories obscure who deaf people are.

It is important to be clear that the Deaf Legal Dilemma is not simply a problem to be resolved through better classification, but a call to rethink how equality law constructs its subjects. Any future legal framework that hopes to recognise deaf people justly must start from the premise that language, culture, and community matter, and that deaf people are not marginal exceptions within disability law, but a collective whose existence demands structural change. Recognition cannot be an act of translation into legal terms deaf people never chose. It must begin with a willingness to listen, or more precisely, to see, deaf people on their own terms.

The next natural step is to propose a solution to the Deaf Legal Dilemma. I offer the Deaf Rights Model. It brings together all the models discussed in this chapter. For too long the law and legal systems have attempted to group deaf individuals into a single model, ignoring the diversity of deaf experience inevitably excluding certain groups or communities of deaf people. This Deaf Rights Model is visually represented in Figure 4.1.

At its core is the intersection of the five distinct but overlapping models covered in this chapter: disability, language minority, culturo-linguistic, ethnic group, and Indigenous group. These models are not mutually exclusive, nor do they fully capture the deaf experience in isolation, but at their intersection lies a more holistic and nuanced understanding of deaf identity. The central space represents this convergence, encapsulating the idea that deaf people's legal status must be drawn from multiple frameworks rather than be confined to one binary choice.

Surrounding these are cross-cutting dimensions – cultural, linguistic, minority, political, and intersectionality – that shape, influence, and mediate how each

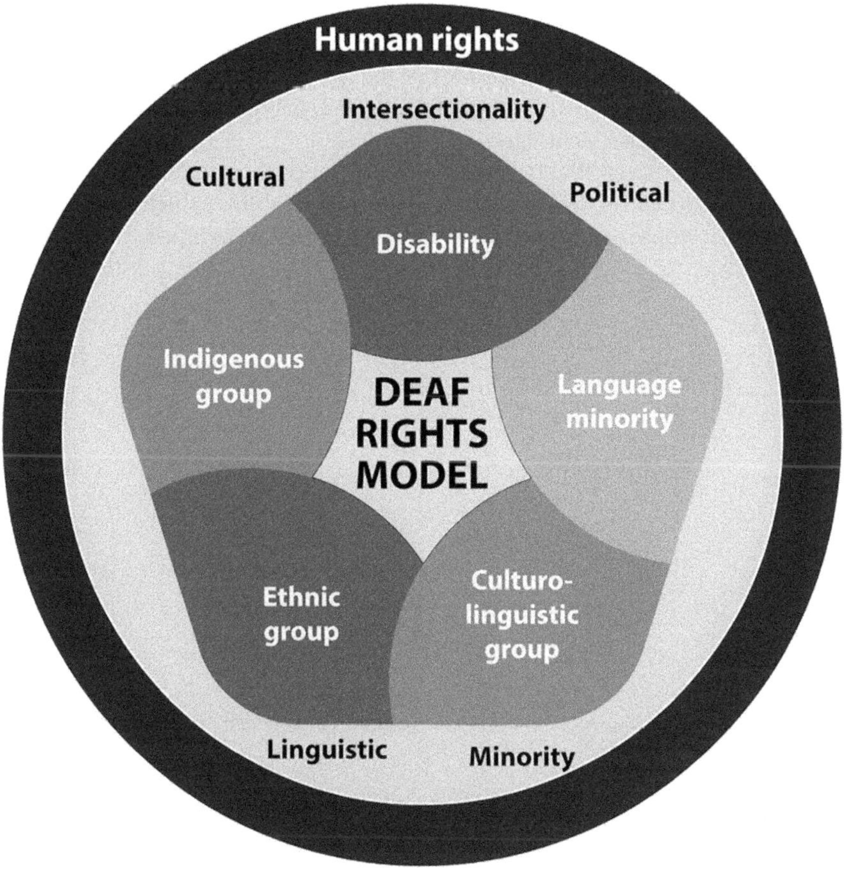

Figure 4.1 The Deaf Rights Model

model is experienced and applied. The cultural and minority models reflect the influence of disability models, but also stand on their own: deaf people share a distinct culture and form a minority group in society. Regardless of their legal status, deaf people's linguistic identities through sign languages are also pervading. Deaf people too are at the mercy of politicians and political systems in general, and their lobbying power will determine what rights they will be given. Finally, intersectionality takes into account the multiple identities that any one deaf individual can have, and while the Deaf Rights Model will predominantly cater for their deaf identity, it also accommodates other identities such as disability, race, nationality, religion, age, LGBTQI+, deaf+ identities.

Enveloping the models and the cross-cutting dimensions is the outermost layer of human rights, as every deaf individual invariably has such rights. While the human rights model of disability is clearly relevant, there are also human rights instruments that protect deaf individuals as a language minority. The human rights layer does not override the dimensions or the models beneath it, but provides a broader framework for their legal implementation, and grounds the deaf experience in existing human rights law.

Together, the Deaf Rights Model offers a conceptual framework for legal reform, one that centres deaf people not as exceptions within a single category, but as a collective requiring interwoven, multi-dimensional recognition.

5

The Deaf Equality Concepts

The legal framing of equality has proven itself to be both conceptually limited and practically ineffective in the lives of deaf people. As the preceding chapters have shown, deaf people are rarely recognised on their own terms: instead, they are categorised, managed, or included only insofar as they conform to frameworks designed by and for others. Yet despite this, the language of equality remains powerful. It continues to shape policies, public debates, and the ways in which deaf people are perceived, and often misrecognised.

This chapter responds not by abandoning the equality framework altogether, but by reclaiming and reimagining it by identifying and applying the Deaf Rights Model. If equality law has failed to protect, what might equality look like if deaf people themselves defined its core concepts? What would it mean to take deaf lives, deaf knowledge, and deaf experiences as the starting point, not the exception, when thinking about fairness, inclusion, dignity, and justice?

The Deaf Equality Concepts that follow do not offer a new legal formula. Instead, they present a reframing: a way of thinking about equality that is rooted in sign language, cultural legitimacy, and epistemic authority. These are not abstract ideals: they are grounded in practice, resistance, and survival.

The first step in this endeavour is to identify which equality concepts are most relevant to deaf people. Equality law has been shaped with specific equality outcomes in mind, so to understand why the law may be failing certain groups, it is important to understand the philosophical assumptions underpinning these laws. If you remember, Vickers argues that 'different analyses of equality may be suited to different protected grounds'[1] while Fraser suggests that 'class inequality is best understood in terms of redistribution, and sexual orientation inequality best understood in terms of recognition'.[2] The aim of this chapter, then, is to explore these theoretical discussions and identify which analyses of equality may be suited to deaf people.

Within Deaf Studies, much of the discourse has centred on discrimination,[3] dignity,[4] social inclusion[5] and challenging oppression, particularly in the form of

[1] Lucy Vickers, 'Promoting Equality or Fostering Resentment? The Public Sector Equality Duty and Religion and Belief' (2011) 31 *Legal Studies* 135, 152.

[2] Nancy Fraser, 'From Redistribution to Recognition? Dilemmas of Justice in a "post-Socialist" Age' in Jeffrey C Alexander and Steven Seidman (eds), *The New Social Theory Reader*, 2nd edn (Routledge, 2008) 68.

[3] Sarah CE Batterbury-Magill, 'The Legal Status of BSL and ISL' (2014), https://bda.org.uk/wp-content/uploads/2017/03/BDA_Legal-status-of-BSL-ISL_11-Mar-2014.pdf.

[4] Harlan L Lane, Robert Hoffmeister and Ben Bahan, *A Journey into the Deaf-World* (DawnSignPress, 1996) 419–20.

[5] Batterbury-Magill (n 3).

audism.[6] Therefore, the concepts of equality relevant to deaf people include equal treatment, equal worth and dignity, social inclusion, and the challenge to oppression. Equality of opportunity is also relevant as, according to Schaar, it is popular with politicians, businessmen, social theorists, and freedom marchers.[7] Equality of outcome is also often used as a test for whether opportunity has in fact been realised and therefore should be included.[8] Finally, full participation, a central tenet of transformative equality,[9] also belongs in this list. These concepts of equality are referred to henceforth as the Deaf Equality Concepts. Underpinning these Deaf Equality Concepts remain the precepts of equality: formal, substantive and transformative, defined in chapter two.

To illustrate how these concepts might play out in practice, I introduce a fictional yet realistic character: Kiran. Kiran lives in a society where equality exists on paper but is inconsistently applied. Kiran comes from a hearing family, with two hearing parents and a hearing sibling. They are married to a deaf individual who is a child of deaf adults. Together, they have three children: the eldest is hearing, and the two youngest are deaf. The family is bilingual, using both sign language and a spoken language. Kiran attended mainstream schools with access to a deaf resource base throughout their formative years and completed higher education with a focus on social justice and policy.

Professionally, Kiran works as an advocate for a non-governmental organisation focused on sign language rights, accessibility and social justice. Their work involves interacting with a wide range of people, organisations, and services, both deaf and hearing, allowing them to witness firsthand how equality laws and systemic structures impact diverse groups, including deaf individuals. Kiran operates in a mid-sized urban area with a diverse population that reflects the global majority. Although a legal framework for equality and disability rights exists, it is inconsistently implemented, posing ongoing challenges. Kiran's experiences – personal, educational, and professional – will be drawn upon to explore what these equality concepts mean when grounded in a deaf context.

It is important to also consider matters through an intersectional lens. To help expose how overlapping identities shape deaf people's experiences of inequality, I introduce a group of individuals; all deaf, but each with an additional identity that complicates how they are seen, supported, or sidelined. We meet Amira, a non-signing deaf professional; Zion, a Black deaf student; Riley, a trans-neurodivergent deaf person; Jayden, a language-deprived deaf adult; Sasha, a deafblind person; Nadia, a South Asian deaf woman; Tama, a Māori deaf community organiser; and Leo, a queer, deaf youth worker. Their stories are not exceptions or extremes; they reflect the complexity and richness of deaf lives and help drive the arguments home.

[6] H-Dirksen L Bauman, 'Audism: Exploring the Metaphysics of Oppression' (2004) 9 *Journal of Deaf Studies and Deaf Education* 239.

[7] John Schaar, 'Equality of Opportunity, and Beyond' in John W Chapman and J Roland Pennock (eds), *Equality* (Atherton Press, 1967) 163.

[8] Anne Phillips, 'Defending Equality of Outcome' [2004] *Journal of Political Philosophy* 1, 10.

[9] Vickers (n 1) 147.

This chapter brings everything together. It draws on the issues, concepts and models introduced so far and reshapes them from a deaf perspective. The aim is not just to revisit earlier ideas, but to reframe them into something coherent and forward-looking. I return to the factors that sit alongside the Deaf Legal Dilemma: charity and the patriarchy, colonialism, cultural competence, the decline of deaf communities, education, information, communication and access, intersectionality, and unconscious bias. I also engage with the different ways equality has been framed – that is, formal, substantive and transformative – and explore how deaf people are positioned across a range of models: the five disability models, the language minority model, and the three cultural models (culturo-linguistic, ethnic, and Indigenous).

This matters because the law has failed to connect these pieces. Equality law is fragmented, reactive, and rarely shaped by the people it claims to protect. By pulling these strands together, I aim to show what equality could look like if deaf people defined its terms. Not by creating a new legal formula, but by shifting the starting point. This chapter uses the Deaf Equality Concepts and applies them to lived experience, framed through the different models and interlocking barriers explored across this book. The examples that follow use the named individuals to show how these concepts might work, or fail, in practice.

I. Equal Treatment

Equal treatment is all about treating 'likes alike'. A working example of equal treatment can be found in the Equality Act 2010 (EqA 2010)'s requirement for a comparator when determining less favourable treatment in direct discrimination cases, and when determining whether an employer has a duty to make reasonable adjustments. If a deaf person is treated the same as a hearing person in any particular situation, then the law assumes that equality has been upheld. The duty to make reasonable adjustments rests on whether the disabled person is put at a substantial disadvantage because of a policy, criterion or practice, physical feature, or the lack of an auxiliary aid, compared to an individual without their disability.

This rather convoluted way of determining whether an individual has been treated equally ignores the structural conditions that resulted in the less favourable treatment, or the substantial disadvantage experienced by the deaf individual in the first place. Equal treatment is all about assuming that sameness is equal to fairness and for deaf people, that assumption will invariably result in inequality.

Kiran often comes across this equal treatment approach. When they try to access a mandatory training session for local authority advocates, the session is held in-person with no interpreter provided. Upon requesting a BSL-English interpreter, the organiser responded: 'We don't provide signers (sic) for anyone else; we treat everyone the same.' On this occasion, equal treatment is used to justify Kiran's exclusion and although Kiran is expected to participate in the training by their employer, it has been mandated, organised and will be delivered by hearing people in a spoken language environment. Their linguistic needs are simply being ignored. If Kiran were to make a claim for direct discrimination, the court would not classify this as such, because in fact, Kiran is not being treated less favourably than any other training attendee, even though it is this equal treatment that is making the actions (or inaction) of the organisers discriminatory in the first place.

If one looks at this situation through a medical model lens, the problem here is Kiran's deafness. They cannot hear, and any barriers they face are because of this simple fact. There is an underlying expectation that they should be able to overcome the barriers with lipreading, note-taking, or simple self-reliance. They should be able to attend and complete the session successfully using these skills, particularly as written resources will be provided and by going through these afterwards Kiran will be able to catch up if they miss anything. The training provider's mindset is not about ensuring that Kiran can participate fully alongside their peers. It reduces participation to information access, not interaction or engagement. There is no consideration of how Kiran may feel in that situation: unable to follow the input from the training leads; unable to join peer discussions; left to awkwardly explain on the day why they will not be participating like everyone else. They will also experience a sense of isolation: they will be excluded socially, professionally, and emotionally. They will not just struggle to learn, they will be sidelined from building professional networks, forming collegial bonds, or being seen as an equal by other advocates.

From a social model angle, the problem lies in the inaccessibility of the training session: the failure to provide a BSL-English interpreter, and the assumption that the language of the session (English) will be sufficient for all the attendees, and that everyone will be able to hear and speak it. Once again, the provider's mindset is still focused on access to materials, not access to participation. The question is not whether Kiran is meaningfully included in the process as a peer, as a professional, or as a person, but whether they will receive the content.

If one uses the culturo-linguistic model instead, a very different question is asked. Why is a public body arranging or delivering training for their employees in a way that ignores BSL as a language? Why is the whole premise excluding deaf BSL signers by default? In other words, the training exists within a monoglot language and cultural framework which centres English as the only legitimate way to communicate. It assumes that everyone hears, speaks and processes information in the same way. It shapes everything: the instructions; the informal discussions; the networking opportunities; the humour; the timing; the flow of questions; the professional interaction. This monoglot language and cultural framework does not just influence the training provider; it runs through the entire infrastructure: the employer who enrolled Kiran on the training; the administrative staff who assumed no interpreters would be needed; the venue team who chose an inaccessible layout; the trainers who designed spoken-only content; and the attendees who unconsciously expect a hearing-subjective space. The culturo-linguistic model reveals this is more than just a one-off oversight; it is a cultural order that renders deaf people, their identity and their language invisible.

The language minority model reframes the situation again, only this time through the lens of rights and legal obligation. It asserts that BSL is not just a communication tool or a cultural asset; it is a minority language that must be recognised, accommodated, and protected under national and international law. From this perspective, Kiran's exclusion is not merely unfortunate: it is a denial of their linguistic rights. Just as a Welsh speaker would have a right to training in their own language in Wales, a BSL signer should have a right to equivalent professional development in BSL. The issue here is not whether the organisers were 'aware' or 'meant well'; it is that they failed to provide for the use of a recognised language of a minority group. Framed this way, the problem is not individual; it is quite simply a failure to comply with the duty to respect and facilitate language rights in public settings.

Meanwhile, Amira, an oral deaf professional hoping to attend the same training as Kiran, is repeatedly told she does not need any adjustments because she can 'speak well'. In meetings, she struggles to follow rapid turn-taking and poor acoustics, but her requests for agendas in advance, real-time captions, or quieter rooms are dismissed as unnecessary. Because she is not a BSL signer, colleagues assume she has no access needs at all and treat her exactly like hearing staff. This rigid 'same treatment' approach erases her actual experience of fatigue, missed content, and constant self-monitoring.

From a medical model perspective, colleagues perceive her ability to speak as evidence that she is 'not really deaf' or has 'overcome' her deafness, reinforcing a deficit lens that equates speech with normality and assumes no support is needed. The social model focuses on adjusting environments but often relies on predefined, standardised fixes such as assuming that 'deaf access' means providing a BSL-English interpreter. Because Amira is oral and does not use BSL, no support is offered at all, and her access needs are overlooked entirely. This reflects how narrow and stereotyped notions of adjustments can exclude those who fall outside dominant deaf identities, reinforcing barriers rather than removing them.

Amira's experience also reveals the limitations of both the culturo-linguistic and language minority models. As an oral deaf professional who communicates in spoken English and does not use BSL, she falls outside the scope of frameworks that centre sign language and cultural affiliation. The culturo-linguistic model typically positions deaf people as a cohesive community defined by shared language and norms, but this does not reflect Amira's identity or experience. Likewise, the language minority model offers little for someone whose access barriers are not rooted in language use. However, this framing assumes that Amira does not use BSL out of choice. Perhaps she was never given the opportunity to acquire it. Her identity could have been shaped within a hearing-dominant world that restricts exposure to sign language through mainstreaming, parental decisions, and educational policy. The very models that claim to protect deaf people may reinforce this exclusion by treating language use as an identity marker rather than a consequence of access.

II. Equality of Opportunity

Equality of opportunity is perhaps the concept that is most widely thought of when one thinks about equality. It is usually framed as ensuring that everyone is at the same starting point for an opportunity that has arisen, such as a job or promotion, and may entail the provision of adjustments or support to level the playing field for those who may have a disadvantage of some sort. In the UK, equality of opportunity forms the bedrock of education and employment policy, with a goal to ensure barriers are removed to enable individuals to compete fairly. However, it is built on the assumption that those barriers are occasional, external, and easily fixed. For deaf people, barriers are often embedded into the very structure of the opportunity itself. The starting point is rarely equal to begin with – the deaf realities highlighted in chapter one – and the law rarely asks why, nor does it take any steps to address these deaf realities.

Kiran sees equality of opportunity most clearly in education. They visit a local secondary school to support a deaf BSL signing teenager who is falling behind. The school insists that 'the same opportunities are available to all students', citing the use of subtitles on videos and a teaching assistant who occasionally signs key words. The student has no regular access to BSL, no deaf peers, and no exposure to deaf adults. When Kiran raises this, a senior leader replies, 'We've treated them exactly the same as everyone else.' They are physically present in the classroom, but linguistically and socially disconnected. Without regular access to BSL, they are left to piece together fragments of spoken English through subtitles or brief gestures. They cannot follow class discussions, join in peer conversations, or ask spontaneous questions. Every interaction requires effort, negotiation, or guesswork. Over time, this erodes their confidence and self-worth. They begin to feel that their language does not belong in school, and by extension, that they do not either. They are not just falling behind academically. They are being pushed out socially, emotionally, and culturally; made to feel that education is something they are allowed to observe, but not fully take part in.

The school's approach appears to be fair, but at the same time reveals just how superficial equality of opportunity can be when it ignores the context in which the student lives: their deaf reality. The issue here is not so much that the adjustments or access have not been made. Instead, it reflects a deeper pattern of Deaf Legal Exclusion: the law that established the education system did not design it with deaf learners in mind. The framework may offer 'equal opportunity' in name, but it was never built with this student as a participant.

From a medical model view, the focus is on the student's hearing loss, and the system's solution to provide individual support, rely on the student's lipreading skills, and to ensure that their speech is improved so that they are able to function in a hearing society. Success is defined as their ability to blend in. The classroom is not expected to change: the child is. If they struggle, the failure is attributed to their own capacity, not to the inadequacy of the environment.

Meanwhile, the social model recognises that the student is being excluded by the school's failure to provide access to the learning environment. It shifts the problem away from the individual and towards the institution, but even then, the solution is often framed in general terms: better acoustics, visual aids, or simplified instructions. It rarely extends to rethinking the cultural or linguistic assumptions that underpin the school itself. What is considered 'access' is still measured against hearing norms. A teaching assistant who signs key words might tick a compliance box, but it does not equate to full, dynamic participation in a BSL-rich environment. The student may be in the room, but the room has not been built with them in mind.

The culturo-linguistic model would consider the school's failure to provide a BSL-rich learning environment and ask why the student's language and identity are absent altogether. Where are the other BSL signers? Where are the deaf adults? Where is the validation of their identity as something to be respected, not overcome? The language rights model reframes this situation again. It would say that the student has the right to learn in their language and have access to their community, and that failing to provide that is not a gap in opportunity, but a denial of it. Just as Welsh- or Gaelic-speaking students would be entitled to instruction in their language, a signing student should not have to justify or negotiate their presence.

A similar situation arises for Kiran's deaf child. They want to join a local swimming club, but the coach refuses to use gestures or learn any signs: 'We've never had a deaf kid before.' On the surface, this might appear to be a neutral statement of fact, but it quickly becomes a justification for inaction. The club sees itself as open to all, but only on the assumption that everyone fits the hearing norm. No adjustments are made, no visual instructions are provided, and no attempt is made to communicate. Kiran's child is physically present at the pool, but cannot follow instructions, join in peer banter, or understand what is happening. They are left on the edge of the activity – watching, mimicking, and guessing – without ever being fully included. Each model frames the exclusion differently: the medical model blames the child; the social model blames the coach; the culturo-linguistic model asks where the deaf identity is; and the language minority model sees a denial of rights.

Taking intersectionality into account, Zion is a Black deaf student repeatedly placed in lower sets due to 'communication difficulties' and unconscious bias, despite strong academic potential. Teachers report that he 'doesn't engage' or 'struggles to follow', overlooking the fact that he rarely has full access to classroom discussion and is often left without consistent BSL support. When his parents raise concerns, they are told the school is 'doing its best' and that 'Zion is in the right group for his ability.' But Zion knows he is capable of more. He completes work quickly, asks insightful questions when supported, and gets higher marks in subjects where visual learning is prioritised. Yet his placement in lower sets limits his access to challenging content and experienced teachers. Over time, he starts to internalise the low expectations around him. The assumptions made about his ability are shaped not only by how he communicates, but by how he looks. His quietness is read as disengagement, his confidence as defiance, and his need for support as a lack of intelligence. Teachers may not be consciously discriminating, but they are unconsciously filtering his behaviour through racialised norms; norms that see Black boys as disruptive unless they are silent and underperforming unless they are exceptional.

III. Respect for Equal Worth, Dignity and Identity

In a 1994 presentation to the Assistant Secretary General for Human Rights of the United Nations, the World Federation of the Deaf affirmed that deaf people are not accorded equal dignity and 'there are even many who want to get rid of us'.[10] The concept of equal worth and dignity is clearly directly relevant to how deaf lives are recognised, portrayed, and valued in everyday systems.

The concept is foundational to many international human rights instruments, but it plays a surprisingly marginal role in UK domestic law. Where it appears, it is often abstract and largely a moral principle rather than a legal standard. For example, the EqA 2010 allows an individual to claim discrimination by harassment which has the purpose or effect of violating their dignity if that harassment is related to a relevant protected characteristic. But the Act offers no definition of 'dignity,' nor any meaningful guidance. For deaf people, this lack of clarity matters as it is not given enough credence or attention by the law to be meaningfully challenged or defended.

Kiran is admitted to hospital following a car accident. No interpreter is provided, and no communication strategy is put in place. For a week, they are given tuna sandwiches – the only food they recognise – and no one checks whether they want anything different. No staff member attempts to explain the routine or engage with Kiran directly. The assumption is that things are 'fine' because there is no complaint, but Kiran is left to navigate care in complete isolation, unable to ask questions, express preferences, or engage with their own treatment. It is not a lack of food or physical care that undermines their dignity, but the absence of recognition.

The medical model treats deafness as a clinical detail, not a reason to adapt care. As long as Kiran is physically stable, no further attention is given to communication. The social model might identify a lack of accessible practice – no interpreter, no visual support – but it still assumes that the problem is logistical. The culturo-linguistic model would ask why a BSL signer is left to survive in a setting where their language is not present, even in basic interactions. The language minority model reframes this again: it is not about courtesy or effort; it is about the failure to recognise that language rights apply even when the lunch trolley makes its way around the hospital wards.

[10] World Federation of the Deaf, 'Violations of Human Rights' (1993) 14 as cited in Harlan L Lane, Robert Hoffmeister and Ben Bahan, *A Journey into the Deaf-World* (DawnSignPress, 1996) 419.

Riley, a trans, neurodivergent deaf person, attends a series of appointments related to gender-affirming care. At no point is a BSL-English interpreter provided, and no account is taken of their language preferences. The process is already difficult: it involves lengthy assessments, unfamiliar environments, and multiple professionals. For Riley, who is autistic, these interactions are overwhelming. The lack of structure, poor visual communication, and unpredictability of the appointments add layers of stress and confusion. Instructions are unclear. Forms are rushed. Questions are repeated in different ways without explanation. No one asks how Riley processes information or whether they need time to respond. On top of this, the process remains highly medicalised and pathologising. Riley is expected to justify their gender identity repeatedly, but is not given the language access or sensory space to do so safely. Healthcare staff focus on their deafness as a 'barrier', but overlook the compounded impact of inaccessible language, clinical environments, and neurodivergent processing needs.

The medical model dominates entirely: it frames Riley's gender identity as something to be verified, their deafness as something to accommodate only when necessary, and their neurodivergence as incidental or irrelevant. The social model might flag environmental barriers – the rushed appointments, the poor communication – but it lacks the tools to account for how these barriers interact across identities.

IV. Equality of Results and Equality of Outcomes

Often dismissed as being unfair or unrealistic, equality of outcome is one of the few concepts of equality that exposes whether equality works, especially for deaf people. While equality of opportunity focuses on ensuring everyone is at the same starting point, equality of outcomes focuses on the end result. It asks whether individuals and groups are achieving desired outcomes in fields such as education, employment, health and justice, and is where gaps can be at their most glaring.

Kiran supports a deaf young adult appealing a Personal Independence Payment refusal. The tribunal process appears inclusive – an interpreter is booked, and the hearing is technically accessible – but none of the legal documentation is available in BSL. All communication before the hearing is in formal English including the decision letter, the appeal form, the evidence submission, and the scheduling. Deadlines are tight, and the deaf claimant has no legal training and no meaningful explanation of what to expect. Kiran provides support, but they are not a legal adviser, and their involvement depends on chance, not entitlement. The interpreter facilitates communication during the hearing, but the claimant is overwhelmed, uncertain, and unable to respond with clarity. The tribunal rejects the appeal. The system will record this as a fair hearing. Kiran sees it differently: this is an outcome that reflects language and procedural exclusion, not merit.

The medical model is embedded in the legal process itself. It frames deafness as an impairment to be worked around, rather than a reason to adapt the system.

Judges may unconsciously assess the claimant's communication through a deficit lens, interpreting hesitation, confusion, or reliance on an interpreter as signs of unreliability, rather than signs of exclusion. The social model acknowledges barriers such as inaccessible paperwork or rushed hearings, but treats them as practical flaws. The culturo-linguistic model recognises that the process centres hearing norms and excludes signers. The language minority model reframes this entirely: the outcome is unjust not because of overt bias, but because the legal system failed to uphold the claimant's right to engage in their own language.

Jayden, a language-deprived deaf adult applies for supported housing. The local authority sends several letters in dense English, including appointment times, eligibility criteria, and documentation requirements. No one checks comprehension, offers translation, or follows up. They miss an assessment appointment and submit the wrong supporting documents. The application is marked 'closed due to non-engagement'. When they try to reapply, they are told they must go back on the waiting list. No one sees this as a failure of the system. To the housing team, the forms were provided. To the applicant, nothing was ever really explained.

The medical model plays a subtle role: Jayden is assumed to be capable of engaging with the system if they're 'not that deaf' or 'can manage independently'. There is no recognition that language deprivation is a long-term consequence of systemic failure, not personal deficit. The social model might highlight communication barriers such as inaccessible letters, lack of follow-up, but still frames them as accidental gaps, not indicators of a wider structural problem. The culturo-linguistic model would ask why the housing service does not recognise BSL as a language or understand that written English may not be fully accessible. The language minority model reframes the entire situation: it is not a failure to provide help, but a failure to recognise the applicant's language rights in navigating essential public services.

V. Social Inclusion

The sixth deaf equality concept is social inclusion, often invoked as a desirable end state, that is, a society where all individuals are able to participate fully, equally, and without discrimination. In reality, however, it is often manifested in terms of physical access to spaces, tokenistic gestures toward 'equality, diversity and inclusion', or superficial representation. The general assumption is that inclusion can be achieved simply by allowing individuals entry, for example, by inviting individuals to apply for jobs and guaranteeing interviews through the Disability Confident employer scheme.[11] For deaf people, however, such initiatives are often regarded as a smokescreen. On the surface, employers may appear to be providing 'access' to jobs, but it does not reassure deaf applicants that they will not experience audism

[11] GOV.UK, 'Disability Confident Employer Scheme' (24 April 2024), www.gov.uk/government/collections/disability-confident-campaign.

once they enter the recruitment space, as audist attitudes and stereotypical views of deaf people may prevail.

For example, deaf people may be welcomed through a charity-based lens, celebrated as 'brave' or 'inspiring' for attending an interview, while the interview itself remains structurally inaccessible. Cultural incompetence within institutions means that sign language access is treated as a luxury or an afterthought. Colonial legacies have established spoken language as the default norm, positioning BSL and other sign languages as deviations to be tolerated rather than languages to be respected. The result is a system that praises itself for inviting deaf people to the table, while consistently failing to redesign the table in ways that enable genuine participation.

Kiran attends a close friend's wedding. The speeches go on for nearly 15 minutes and guests laugh, cry, and applaud. No interpreter has been arranged, and no transcript or summary was provided. Kiran sits smiling politely, aware that they are excluded from one of the most meaningful parts of the ceremony. When they raise it gently later, the bride says, 'We didn't even think, but you looked like you were enjoying it!' The social model recognises that the lack of access – no interpreter, no transcript – prevented inclusion, but still treats the solution as a personal accommodation rather than a collective responsibility. The culturo-linguistic model sees the wedding as a hearing-centred event that unconsciously excludes sign language and deaf ways of relating. The language rights model points to a deeper absence: the absence of planning, awareness, and commitment to language inclusion even in informal spaces.

A local health board invites Kiran to join a local equality panel that focuses on improving accessibility in health services. The organiser is enthusiastic: 'We're so glad to have your perspective,' they say. But when Kiran attends the first online meeting, the BSL-English interpreter has not been booked. The livestream captions are automated and riddled with errors. Kiran is present in name, but not in language. They remain silent for much of the discussion, aware that their inclusion is symbolic rather than transformative.

Each model frames this differently. The medical model sees Kiran's deafness as the barrier and imagines lipreading, confidence, or assertiveness as solutions, locating the problem in the individual. The social model blames the lack of adjustments, but still assumes inclusion means helping someone access a space designed by others. The culturo-linguistic model challenges why the space was not designed with BSL signers in mind at all, reframing inclusion as cultural redesign, not technical fix. The language rights model sees a violation of language equality: Kiran was denied the right to be included in their own language.

Sasha, a deafblind activist, is invited to join the same local equality panel as Kiran. The organisers are eager to highlight their inclusive approach. A BSL-English interpreter is present at an in-person meeting, and automated captions are turned on on a screen. But Sasha uses tactile sign language and requires guiding support, neither of which have been arranged. They are seated alone at the edge of the room, no one checks in with them, and no one realises that the 'interpreter' is inaccessible to them. When feedback is requested at the end, Sasha is listed as 'in attendance'.

The social model sees Sasha's exclusion as a failure of access provision but still frames the solution in terms of bolt-on adjustments. The culturo-linguistic model asks why the concept of inclusion failed to recognise the diversity within deaf communities, and why sign language provision was treated as a universal fix. The language rights model argues that inclusion must be rooted in meaningful inclusion and that this includes planning for tactile modes, alternative formats, and shared decision-making with those affected.

VI. Challenging oppression

What pervades deaf people's experiences within society at large is oppression; the ways in which systems actively marginalise and silence deaf people. Challenging oppression means naming and confronting power. It shifts the frame from 'how can we include you?' to 'why were we excluded in the first place, and who benefits from that?' Kiran faces this directly when a major charity launches a public awareness campaign promoting 'early intervention' for deaf children. The message implies that with the right technology and therapy, deaf children can become 'as normal as possible.' The underlying assumption is clear: spoken language is the goal, sign language is a fallback, and deaf culture is invisible. When Kiran questions this framing, they are accused of being divisive and told that 'this is about helping families, not politics.' The charity is seen as benevolent. Kiran is seen as hostile. But what they're challenging is not kindness; it is control.

The medical model is doing most of the heavy lifting here. Deafness is framed as a deficit to be fixed, and 'help' is defined on hearing terms. The social model would criticise the lack of systemic adjustments but may not go far enough in naming the cultural erasure at work. The culturo-linguistic model recognises what is missing: deaf identity, community, and sign language as a legitimate choice not a consolation. The language rights model would argue that deaf children and families have the right to information, to sign language, and to cultural belonging, and that withholding these is not neutral, but oppressive.

Tama is a friend of Kiran's, whom they met at a World Federation of the Deaf Congress a few years ago. Based in Aotearoa, Tama, a Māori deaf community organiser, challenges the framing of a national deaf mental health campaign that ignores Indigenous perspectives. He advocates for the inclusion of Māori models of wellbeing such as *whānau* (family/kinship), *wairua* (spiritual connection), and *mana* (inherent dignity), but is told that the campaign must stay 'neutral' and 'scientific.' Shortly after, he is dropped from the advisory panel with no explanation. While the culturo-linguistic and language minority models offer some recognition for signers, they have not yet engaged meaningfully with Indigenous frameworks. An Indigenous group model would start somewhere else entirely: with relationships, responsibilities, land, and culture. It would see Tama's knowledge as central, not disruptive. Tama's case shows how equality law does not just fail to recognise his deaf identity or his Indigeneity, it fails to recognise that these identities are inseparable, and that their intersection creates forms of exclusion the law simply is not built to see.

Nadia is a South Asian deaf woman studying at college. She is confident in her identity, uses BSL fluently, and wears hijab as part of her faith. During her first term, she begins to experience targeted bullying and harassment. A group of students mock her signing, imitating her gestures and pulling exaggerated faces. Clips of her using BSL are filmed without consent and edited with fake subtitles to make her appear incoherent or ridiculous. In class, one student mutters 'terrorist' under their breath when she asks a question. Another comments that she always gets 'special treatment' when she arrives with her communication support worker. When Nadia raises concerns with her tutor, the response is sympathetic but evasive: 'It's hard to control what happens outside lessons.' No action is taken. The behaviour escalates. Nadia begins to miss classes and eventually transfers to a different college.

This is not simply a case of individual bullying. It is racialised audism: a convergence of racism, linguistic marginalisation, sexism, and religious stereotyping. The harm Nadia experiences is not only interpersonal but structural. Her signing is not recognised as a legitimate language but mocked as a spectacle. Her presence as a hijab-wearing, signing woman is seen as too visible, too political, too different. She is punished not for disrupting the classroom, but for existing in it.

The medical model reduces her distress to an individual vulnerability, implying she may need emotional support or adjustments to cope. The social model acknowledges the institution's failure to protect her but frames it as a gap in inclusive practice rather than a reflection of embedded bias. The culturo-linguistic model reveals how BSL is treated not as a valued minority language, but as something alien or entertaining, its public expression open to mockery. The language minority model points to the denial of Nadia's right to learn, communicate, and participate through her language in a safe environment. But it is the ethnic group model that offers the most complete framing. Nadia is not excluded simply because she is deaf, or Asian, or a woman but because the intersection of these identities makes her unintelligible to systems built around Whiteness, speech, and hearing norms. The dominant culture of the college, including its deaf spaces, positions Whiteness and English fluency as defaults. When Nadia does not conform, her exclusion is minimised, and her departure framed as a personal decision rather than a failure of institutional responsibility.

VII. Full Participation

Of all the concepts of equality, full participation is perhaps the most transformative, and the most routinely denied to deaf people. Participation is often misunderstood as mere presence: being in the room, being consulted, being counted. But full participation means more than visibility. It means having power, influence, and agency. It means shaping the systems individuals are part of, not simply being allowed to observe them.

Lane argues that deaf people do not generally have the 'chance at self-creating to the best of his or her abilities', and should be crucial participants in the discussion and agreement concerning the lives of deaf children and adults, and the roles of the professions that serve them. They have been excluded by law and by oppressive education, by statute or connivance from the education of most deaf children. Their counsel, which is needed by the parent of a newborn deaf child more than any other, is excluded from the home and the clinic. Their services as a language model for the deaf child are eschewed and the responsibility unconscionably given to the children's hearing family, who cannot fulfil it. Indeed, their very existence is all but denied. They are not participants in the programmes of research on deaf people, and they are merely the passive objects of that research. Their role in programmes that provide services to deaf people is severely restricted.[12]

Kiran hears that one of their children's favourite bands is going on tour and wants to go with their children. When booking the tickets, they contact the promoter to request a BSL-English interpreter. At first, the request is dismissed – 'We don't usually get asked for that' – and they are advised to book tickets and 'see what happens'. After repeated follow-up emails, the promoter eventually agrees to provide an interpreter, but offers no confirmation and stops responding. Kiran books the tickets anyway. On the day of the concert, they arrive to find there is no interpreter. The support acts have already started, and no access has been arranged. Staff seem unsure what to do. Kiran is told: 'There might be someone coming later.' Eventually, a BSL interpreter arrives for the main act, but they are positioned side-stage with no spotlight, difficult to see from Kiran's seat, and not introduced or acknowledged. The interpreter leaves before the encore, and none of the support acts were interpreted. Kiran's children enjoy themselves, singing and dancing all evening, but Kiran could not follow much of what was happening. The whole experience felt like an afterthought. What was meant to be a shared night out becomes another reminder that deaf people are welcome in principle, but not in practice.

From a medical model perspective, the issue lies in Kiran's deafness; the assumption being that concerts are naturally difficult for deaf people, and limited access is just something to be expected. The social model reframes the problem as a failure to provide appropriate adjustments: the late, partial interpreter provision; the poor visibility; the lack of planning. The culturo-linguistic model goes further, asking why deaf audience members are always expected to adapt to hearing spaces, rather than expecting events to be designed with signers in mind. The language rights model frames it as a denial of equal cultural participation; a failure to uphold the right to access public life in one's own language.

[12] Harlan Lane, *The Mask of Benevolence: Disabling the Deaf Community* (Alfred A Knopf 1992) 23.

Leo, a queer deaf youth worker, is invited to join a public arts commission exploring young people's experiences of identity and belonging. The organisers are enthusiastic: 'We're so excited to have your voice at the table; your perspective is exactly what we need.' But from the first meeting, it is clear that access has not been properly planned. The agenda and background papers are emailed late in dense, jargon-filled English. No BSL-English interpreter has been arranged. When Leo raises this, the chair apologises and says, 'We just didn't think. We'll do better next time.' At the second meeting, a signer is present but arrives late and leaves early due to scheduling issues. Leo tries to make points throughout the discussion but is often interrupted or overlooked. The conversation moves quickly, with jokes and shorthand references that rely on shared cultural assumptions. When the draft recommendations are circulated, Leo's ideas appear, but without attribution. Some of their more critical suggestions, especially around intersectional access and queer youth spaces, have been softened or omitted. When they flag this, the chair responds: 'We've tried to balance all the views; we didn't want to be too political.' At publication, Leo is listed as a contributor, but feels their role was symbolic, not substantive.

From a medical model perspective, Leo's deafness is treated as the primary issue, with any exclusion seen as unfortunate but outside the organisers' control. The social model focuses on the practical barriers: poor preparation, lack of access, limited support, but still frames inclusion as a matter of adjustments. The culturo-linguistic model highlights the deeper problem: the space was designed without deaf norms, visual language, or cultural fluency in mind. But Leo's queerness also shapes their experience. The panel treats their identity as a welcome addition, but not as a knowledge base. Their intersectional insights as someone navigating marginalisation on multiple fronts are dismissed as too political or disruptive. The language rights model reframes this as a denial of language legitimacy.

VIII. Conclusion

This chapter has reimagined what equality could mean if deaf people defined it. Instead of trying to fix deaf people to fit existing systems, the Deaf Equality Concepts ask what those systems might look like if they were built with deaf lives in mind from the start. Each concept – equal treatment, equal opportunity, equal worth and dignity, equality of outcome, social inclusion, full participation, and the need to challenge oppression – expose how narrow and conditional current interpretations of equality remain. Taken together, they offer a more grounded, more demanding, and more truthful account of deaf people need.

The law still treats equality as something that can be measured in procedures: a comparator, a policy, an adjustment. But as Kiran, Amira, Zion, Riley, Sasha, Nadia, Leo and Tama each show, equality is not experienced in abstract terms. It is experienced in classrooms, clinics, courts, concerts, and community spaces where language, identity and power intersect. Legal frameworks often miss this entirely. They treat access as technical, oppression as accidental, and participation as passive. In doing so, they reduce deaf people to cases, not contributors.

By drawing on multiple models – the medical, social, culturo-linguistic, language minority, ethnic, and Indigenous – this chapter has not sought to replace one frame with another, but to highlight their limitations and possibilities. No single model captures the whole picture. What matters is who is doing the framing and what is still being left out.

The Deaf Equality Concepts do not offer a new formula. They are not a checklist or a test. They are a shift in starting point. They begin with deaf people's knowledge, deaf people's language, and deaf people's ways of being. They call out the gap between symbolic inclusion and lived exclusion. And they do not ask to be invited in; they ask why the system was designed without deaf people in the room at all.

What becomes clear from these case studies is that while existing equality models each offer partial insights, none adequately address the Deaf Legal Dilemma. The characters' experiences – Kiran's rejection, Aliya's frustration, and Tama's conditional inclusion – point to the need for a new model. The Deaf Rights Model, introduced in the previous chapter, seeks to respond to these realities not by tweaking existing frameworks, but by reframing deaf identity, rights, and recognition on their own terms.

If equality continues to be something done to deaf people, it will continue to fall short. But if it is redefined by deaf people themselves on their own terms, vis-a-vis the Deaf Rights Model, then the idea of equality might finally start to mean something real.

6

Beyond the Dilemma

And so, we reach the end of this book. I hope that its effect has been profound, and your eyes opened to the lived experience of deaf individuals navigating legal systems. Deaf people are not a homogenous group and there is no single experience that speaks for all of us. But there are patterns. These patterns are often deep-rooted, recurring and structural, and many of us come against these again and again.

Against a backdrop of paternalistic dominance and a sometimes overpowering need to 'look after' deaf people through a 'deficit' model, hearing societies have long imposed their norms by sponsoring medical interventions, providing financial compensation through social security initiatives, and pressuring deaf individuals via education systems and the labour market. This attempt to assimilate neglects deaf individuals' identity and cultural practices in legal systems and maintains the status quo: that deaf people are on the margins of society as a group of people who do not quite fit.

One could argue that this is not society's intention, which is true to a certain extent, as this patriarchy took root through human evolution because of economic and technological factors, but the question is: does society maintain the status quo even when it knows or recognise that its actions may be seen to be patriarchal? If it does, then perhaps this is audist colonialism in action? Are the colonisers – hearing society – imposing their norms and their culture on deaf people without their consent?

This paternal and colonial tendency means that many service providers, employers, and law- and policymakers lack the cultural competence to work with and to include deaf individuals. Is unconscious bias at play here? Are members of hearing society making automatic judgements about the deaf individuals they encounter in their day-to-day lives, or if they are in positions of authority or influence, of deaf people at large?

Alongside, or perhaps even because of, this colonialism, deaf communities are in decline. Deaf spaces once flourished in most cities and towns but are now reduced to a small number. This means that intergenerational connections are not always possible, and deaf individuals find it difficult to locate and access deaf communities, preventing them from fully immersing themselves in deaf culture and language. This decline in deaf spaces is mirrored in deaf education, where deaf schools are few and far between, and mainstreaming policy does not always cater for deaf children's unique language needs, affecting learning and attainment.

The fallacies of deaf education compound the lack of information prevalent in deaf individuals due to language and communication issues during childhood, resulting in a lack of prior knowledge as they reach adulthood and have to contend with situations that assume they have a contextual understanding of that particular situation. Access can go some way towards addressing these gaps in knowledge, but the very idea of 'access' is also problematic, and it has been referred to as an 'illusion of inclusion'[1] and an 'institutionally normative'[2] solution.

Above all, the intersectionality of deaf individuals is largely ignored by law- and policymakers. They are not able to get things right for them, and so it seems to be unlikely that they can deal with the disadvantages faced by deaf people with additional marginalised identities such as race, gender, sexual orientation and disability.

With those patterns as a backdrop, this book has delved into equality: what it is; what it hopes to achieve; how it works in practice; and how it should work in practice. You should now have a clearer understanding of, first, the fallacy of formal and substantive equality and the potential of transformative equality to effect change, and second, within the UK context, how the European Convention on Human Rights ('the Human Rights Convention'), the United Nations Convention on the Rights of Persons with Disabilities ('the Disability Convention'), and the Equality Act 2010 (EqA 2010) each manifest these precepts of equality.

You should also realise that deaf people are not just disabled, as equality law generally treats them, but there are convincing arguments for them to be considered a language minority, a culturo-linguistic group, an ethnic group, and an Indigenous group. Yet the law, by and large, does not do so. Instead, the Deaf Legal Dilemma comes to the fore: to be recognised, they are forced to misidentify themselves.

To seek redress from inequality and discrimination, they must rely on legal categories that ignore their deafhood, their culture, and their language. To make matters worse, the law does not recognise their culturo-linguistic, ethnic, or Indigenous status. It may recognise their language minority status, but this is often prescribed outside of language minority frameworks that prioritise spoken languages, and is therefore treated as different, and persist within disability frameworks.

What I do next is quite radical: I take a set of fictional deaf characters – Kiran, Amira, Zion, Riley, Sasha, Nadia, Leo and Tama –who undoubtedly exist in some form in the real world and are grounded in realities that are all too familiar. Because legal systems rarely allow deaf people to present their experiences on their own terms, I have used fiction to reclaim that space. I provide examples of their daily struggles and the impact of those struggles and consider them from a number of

[1] Maartje De Meulder and Hilde Haualand, 'Sign Language Interpreting Services: A Quick Fix for Inclusion?' (2019) 16 *Translation and Interpreting Studies* 19.

[2] Maartje De Meulder and Hilde Haualand, 'Sign Language Interpreting Services: A Quick Fix for Inclusion?' (World Association of Sign Language Interpreters Conference, Paris, France, 15 July 2019).

angles: the concepts of equality that are most relevant to deaf people (what I call the Deaf Equality Concepts), the different models or groupings, and test, challenge and reimagine how equality might work in those situations. This exercise is more than academic. It aims to test the law's assumptions, expose its limitations, and reimagine how equality might operate if deaf people were not asked to misidentify themselves to the law, but if the law was reshaped to fit them. It shows how getting the framing right can have a positive effect and serves as a lesson and way forward for law- and policymakers to improve equality outcomes for deaf people.

As I conclude this book, I briefly recap the main concepts and arguments developed throughout, and then decisively consider the limits and future role of formal, substantive and transformative equality. I offer suggestions for how lawmakers, policymakers, researchers, and others can move forward with the knowledge this book has set out, and I consider the role that Deaf Legal Theory might play in that process. I then deliver a call to action and put forward proposals on what should be done next.

I. Framing Equality

The British Deaf Association's mission is to enhance freedom, equality and diversity for deaf people.[3] This is all well and good, but in order to really understand what equality for deaf people looks like – what it hopes to achieve, how it works in practice; and how it should work in practice – it was necessary to take a deep dive into the theories and concepts of equality. This was a significant undertaking, and as Hellman and Moreau point out, one of the reasons equality law remains such a difficult field is that scholars cannot even agree on the most important questions to ask.[4] Current debates tend to split between technical, doctrinal work on discrimination law, philosophical explorations of equality as a value, and discussions of policies like affirmative action.[5] There is no shortage of academic literature, ranging from abstract theorising to detailed legal analysis at national, European and international levels,[6] but too often, these conversations happen in silos, disconnected from the lived realities they aim to address.

I narrow this exploration of equality to seven concepts of equality. Equal treatment manifests itself as treating likes alike and directly comparing the treatment of a complainant with an actual or hypothetical individual or individuals without the particular characteristic. Meanwhile, equality of opportunity is viewed as creating the necessary conditions to ensure a fair and equal starting point for

[3] British Deaf Association, 'What We Stand For' (2025), https://bda.org.uk/history/what-we-stand-for.

[4] Deborah Hellman and Sophia Moreau, *Philosophical Foundations of Discrimination Law* (Oxford University Press, 2015) 872.

[5] ibid.

[6] Dagmar Schiek, Lisa Waddington and Mark Bell, *Cases, Materials and Text on National, Supranational and International Non-Discrimination Law* (Hart Publishing, 2007) vii.

all, and equality of outcome to eliminate disadvantages faced by particular social groups.[7] In terms of their relationship to each other, Phillips suggests that equality of opportunity is the primary objective of equality, but equality of outcome is the test for identifying whether the objective has been achieved.[8]

Respect for the worth and dignity of each individual is considered a foundation for equality rights and tends to find expression in international treaties rather than domestic anti-discrimination law, essentially requiring that everyone should be treated with respect by each other due to our common humanity. There is an argument that as a concept of equality, social inclusion goes beyond substantive equality, and that discrimination law should be concerned with it instead. Academics[9] who advocate challenging oppression (or audism in the present context) as a concept of equality argue that the theories of justice should attend to the injustice and oppression experienced by groups in decisions relating to distribution. Finally, full participation as a concept is arguably fundamental to achieving social equality.

The next stage was to take a step back and think about standards of measurement or effectiveness for each of those concepts of equality, a way of categorising these concepts of equality. Westen explains that equality is sometimes used as a form of shorthand to refer to certain precepts about equality, that is, certain normative axioms whose truth is said to be inherent in or follow from the concept of equality.[10] This contrasts with concepts of equality, which effectively particularise the precepts. The concepts of formal, substantive and transformative equality therefore became 'categories' or 'precepts', and it was possible to extrapolate which categories each concept of equality was more likely to fit into.

Therefore, equal treatment and equality of opportunity are concepts of equality associated with formal equality, and I argue that they have exhausted their usefulness. Substantive equality includes respect for equal worth and dignity, eliminating discrimination, and equality of outcome and results. I argue that they are too reactive. Transformative equality, which includes social inclusion, challenging oppression and full participation, are in reality rarely implemented and more an ideal than real. This exercise means that you should now have a clearer understanding of, first, the fallacy of formal and substantive equality and the potential of transformative equality to effect change.

II. The Deaf Legal Illusion

The Deaf Legal Illusion pulls back the curtain on how law claims to protect deaf people while structurally failing them. Despite equality legislation and human

[7] Colm O'Cinneide, 'Fumbling Towards Coherence: The Slow Evolution of Equality and Anti-Discrimination Law in Britain' (2006) 57 *Northern Ireland Legal Quarterly* 57, 60.

[8] Anne Phillips, 'Defending Equality of Outcome' [2004] *Journal of Political Philosophy* 1, 14.

[9] Such as Elizabeth C Anderson, Samuel Scheffler, Colm O'Cinneide and Irene M Young.

[10] Peter Westen, *Speaking of Equality: An Analysis of the Rhetorical Force of Equality in Moral and Legal Discourse* (Princeton University Press, 1990) 181.

rights frameworks that appear to offer safeguards, the reality is far murkier. This chapter takes the reader through key legal instruments: the Human Rights Convention, the Disability Convention, and the EqA 2010, and interrogates how they function (or malfunction) in relation to deaf people's lived experiences.

At first glance, these instruments may seem inclusive. But on closer inspection, they are built on frameworks that either erase deaf identity altogether or subsume it under a medicalised understanding of disability. The EqA's focus on reasonable adjustments is symbolic more than substantive, placing the burden on individuals to navigate systems not built for them. Similarly, Article 14 of the Human Rights Convention is not a standalone right, and its utility is limited unless paired with another breached right. The Disability Convention, meanwhile, lacks teeth: while its language is promising, enforcement mechanisms are weak and largely symbolic.

Legal victories are rare and often require deaf people to misrepresent themselves to fit legal categories that were never designed with them in mind. What becomes apparent is that the law demands conformity rather than recognising diversity. At every turn, the onus is on the individual deaf person to prove they are entitled to a right, rather than on systems to be proactively inclusive.

This chapter exposes how formal and substantive equality, when applied in this legal context, do not go far enough. Rather than transforming structures or enabling full participation, they maintain the status quo under the guise of fairness. As such, the illusion persists: the law appears to be working, but deaf people remain systematically marginalised.

III. The Deaf Legal Dilemma

The legal system claims to offer protection to deaf people, but only on terms that misrepresent who they are. This is the heart of the Deaf Legal Dilemma: to be recognised by equality law, deaf people must first misidentify themselves as disabled. This is not a rejection of the fact that some deaf people are disabled, but a critique of the legal requirement that all deaf people must occupy the category of disability to be protected at all. Law sees deafness as an individual impairment, a lack, a deficit, ignoring the cultural, linguistic, and communal dimensions that are central to deaf identity.

The chapter begins by interrogating the disability models that shape how deaf people are categorised in law: medical, social, minority group, cultural, and human rights models. Each provides partial recognition, but ultimately none manage to see deaf people on their own terms. The medical model requires deaf people to be 'fixed' or 'treated'. The social model identifies social barriers but still treats deafness as a problem to be solved. The minority group model foregrounds rights, but not culture. The cultural model introduces representation, while the human rights model provides an aspirational framework, but they remain rooted in disability discourse.

None of these models escape the deficit framing entirely. Deaf people continue to be constructed as recipients of accommodations rather than members of a distinct culturo-linguistic community. Even sign language laws, where they exist, tend to treat sign language as an accessibility tool rather than as a legitimate language in its own right. BSL signers, for instance, are the only non-English speakers who must invoke disability law to access services in their first language.

To move beyond this dilemma, the chapter explores alternative framings. What happens when deaf people are understood as a language minority, or as a culturo-linguistic group? What if deaf identity is conceptualised as an ethnic identity, or even as Indigenous? These framings are not without difficulty, especially in legal terms, but they begin from the right place: the values, practices, and epistemologies of deaf communities themselves.

Each alternative model, whether grounded in shared language, community institutions, or intergenerational socialisation, offers a way of understanding deaf identity that moves beyond the binary of normal/abnormal, ability/disability. It invites law to stop asking deaf people to conform to categories they never chose and instead begin seeing deaf people on their own terms.

This chapter does not propose a perfect solution. Rather, it exposes the poverty of the current legal approach and introduces a conceptual tool, The Deaf Rights Model, to rethink how the law might do better. At its core, it is a call to move from legal accommodation to legal recognition; from managing deaf people to respecting them.

IV. Future Directions

A. For Legal Reform

Equality law is not working for deaf people. There needs to be a shift in how legal protections are conceptualised and implemented. Current provisions often fall short, either because they reflect a narrow understanding of equality or because their mechanisms are too weak to challenge oppression. Below, I outline key areas of reform, each aligned with one of the equality concepts explored earlier in the book.

i. Strengthening Reasonable Adjustment Duties

The reasonable adjustments duty under the EqA 2010 should be reformed to ensure that recurrent adjustments (such as regular interpreter provision) are just as likely to be considered reasonable as single, one-off adjustments.

When an adjustment is needed to prevent human rights infringements under the Human Rights Act 1998 (HRA 1998), they are more likely to be provided. However, if not, an individual cannot make a claim for the failure to make such adjustments alone; they can only do so if another article is infringed. Consideration therefore needs to be given to reform Article 14 of the Human Rights Convention so that it can be claimed as a standalone provision without relying on other article infringements.

If the Council of Europe are unwilling to do so, the HRA 1998 could be amended, without infringing the UK's human rights obligations as signatories of the Human Rights Convention. Article 53 of the Convention allows state parties to offer more generous protections than those provided by the Convention: 'Nothing in this Convention shall be construed as limiting or derogating from any of the human rights and fundamental freedoms which may be ensured under the laws of any High Contracting Party.'

ii. Reforming Enforcement Mechanisms

A major issue in terms of seeking redress for inequality, discrimination or human rights infringements are the difficulties evident in enforcing one's rights. Given the lack of access to legal advice, and the usual caveats associated with litigation, deaf individuals are doomed from the start. It is also not possible to seek redress for contraventions of the Disability Convention, other than through a 'communications' process, and even if the Disability Convention Committee finds in favour of a complainant, the only sanction available is that the Committee will keep the case open until satisfactory measures are taken by the state party.

The public equality sector duty (PSED) has generated some positive outcomes for deaf people, but case law has shown that it can be difficult to challenge public authorities for imposing rules or criteria that disadvantage deaf individuals if the authority offers reasonable compromises. Most PSED case law shows that judgments tend to rest on whether the authority has failed to provide evidence of compliance. In terms of the Disability Convention and state reporting, lack of compliance merely results in a slap on the hand for governments without meaningful sanctions to effect change.

iii. Embedding Sign Language into the Equality Framework

One legislative route would be to embed BSL and Irish Sign Language into the equality framework, perhaps by adding sign language use as a protected characteristic or guaranteeing an absolute right to sign language interpreters, not subject to the reasonableness test. This could be enacted through existing sign language law, such as the BSL (Scotland) Act 2015, the BSL Act 2022, and the imminent BSL (Wales) Act and Sign Language (Northern Ireland) Act.

iv. Reframing Sign Language Rights as Collective Entitlements

Another approach could be to shift from the narrow concept of reasonable adjustments, which focuses on individual accommodations, to a model based on collective entitlements. These are rights or obligations that apply by default to members of a group, without requiring individual requests or justifications. Examples would include the automatic provision of interpreters in public services, the presumption of BSL-English bilingual education policies for deaf children, and systemic language planning measures. This approach would be consistent with existing legal frameworks. Under the EqA 2010, anticipatory duties already exist in some contexts (such as goods and services), and the PSED would create a basis for systemic change. The BSL Act 2022 is still underdeveloped as legislation and could be used to amend the EqA 2010 and education law. These solutions offer a more transformative model of equality, one that removes the burden from the individual to seek adjustments and instead places responsibility on institutions to plan inclusively from the outset.

v. Developing the Deaf Rights Model

There must be a paradigm shift in how the law understands and engages with deaf people. Rather than relying on outdated or narrow models, the law should move towards a new approach to legal recognition, one that acknowledges deaf identity and the intersectional experiences of deaf individuals. This would require a comprehensive review of existing laws to ensure they no longer reflects a medicalised or one-dimensional understanding of being deaf.

The Deaf Rights Model introduced in this book offers a foundation for such a shift. As explored in chapter five, each of the models applied – the disability model, the language minority model, the culturo-linguistic model, the ethnic group model, and the Indigenous group model – capture certain aspects of deaf people's lives, but fall short when taken in isolation. Used individually, these models are partial; together, they reflect the complexity, plurality, and legal invisibility that define many deaf experiences.

Bringing these together into a cohesive legal framework – the Deaf Rights Model – means embracing a transformative and inclusive vision of legal recognition. The Deaf Rights Model is not a prescriptive solution, but a pluralistic foundation that can be shaped by, and with, deaf communities. What this model should look like in practice must be co-created with deaf people across the world, reflecting not only legal theory but lived experience and collective aspirations.

B. For Policy and Practice

i. Deaf Education Reform

It is documented that deaf education is not achieving its desired outcomes, as many deaf children enter education at the age of three with language deprivation.[11]

[11] Lucy Wox, 'The Dignicide of Deaf Children: Is Language Deprivation a Breach of Their Human Rights?' (University of the West of England Bristol, in progress).

Early years education is generally reserved to the private sector, but once diagnosed, deaf children will have access to the education system through audiological interventions and a referral to a Teacher of Deaf Children and Young People.

Therefore, it is possible to end language deprivation, and this can only be done by recognising the right to early bilingual (BSL and English) education for deaf children. A model for this exists in Scotland, whereby the Education (Scotland) Act 2025 puts BSL on an equal footing to Gaelic and requires the newly formed Qualification Scotland to consider the needs of pupils who use BSL or learn in BSL.

In terms of school education, the BSL Curriculum for Primary and Secondary Schools covers key stages 1 to 4 and aims to provide a structured curriculum encompassing the linguistic features, historical context and cultural significance of BSL, ensuring that deaf children can receive a quality education in sign language.[12] This should be integrated into national curricula.[13]

ii. Monolingual Services

A practical step to eliminate or reduce barriers in accessing public services and avoiding the perpetuation of the 'illusion of inclusion' through the provision of sign language interpreters is to introduce 'language-concordant'[14] services; that is, monolingual services whereby a service is delivered in sign language.[15] This would mainly be through providing deaf individuals with employment opportunities and recruiting them to frontline roles. It could also be through training hearing staff to learn the basics of BSL.

iii. Lived Experience in Policymaking

Co-production must be the default position in policymaking. If proposals are made for policy or legal development that will affect deaf people, deaf involvement is key. The aim of co-production is to focus on how to allocate resources and assets within the proposals to achieve better outcomes.[16] The full participation of deaf individuals in these processes will ensure that deaf lived experience is considered and incorporated into policy.

[12] Rob Wilks and Rachel O'Neill, 'Integrating British Sign Language into Deaf Education' (2025) *The Language Learning Journal* 1; BSL Curriculum Working Group, 'British Sign Language Curriculum for Primary and Secondary Schools', https://primarysite-prod-sorted.s3.amazonaws.com/frank-barnes-school-for-deaf-children/UploadedDocument/ce1d304c-f324-4223-9ed7-4d365a7c99bf/bsl-curriculum-final.pdf.

[13] Wilks and O'Neill (n 12).

[14] De Meulder and Haualand (n 2).

[15] Rob Wilks, 'Developing Deaf Jurisprudence: The Role of Interpreters and Translators' in Christopher Stone and others (eds), *Routledge Handbook of Sign Language Translation and Interpreting* (Routledge, 2022) 258.

[16] Carmen Vargas and others, 'Co-Creation, Co-Design, Co-Production for Public Health – a Perspective on Definition and Distinctions' (2022) 32 *Public Health Research & Practice* 1.

C. For Research

i. Develop the Concept of the Deaf Legal Dilemma

In the context of dealing with criticisms of the social model of disability, Oliver posited: '[it would be] far better if critics had spent less of their time criticising the social model for its perceived failures and instead put more effort into attempting to apply it in areas of racism, sexism and homosexuality'.[17] This open-minded approach to future development of the social model of disability has stuck with me ever since, and it resonates in the present context.

This book is not intended to be the definitive article, final presentation or singular interpretation of the Deaf Legal Dilemma and the other concepts I have introduced. It is an opening: an invitation to reflect, respond, and act. It gestures forward, pointing to legal reform, policy innovation, deeper community engagement, and new theoretical models. The next step lies in how this work is taken up by others: by researchers, deaf communities, policymakers, and allies who are willing to think differently about law, justice, and deaf lives.

ii. Establish Deaf Legal Studies as an Interdisciplinary Field

This book opens the door to something broader: the emergence of Deaf Legal Studies as a field in its own right. It is by no means the first piece of work to explore the intersection between deaf people and legal systems,[18] but it is the first to explicitly identify itself as part of this emerging field. By naming and framing Deaf Legal Studies, this book provides a foundation for others to build upon.

As part of the development of the Deaf Legal Studies movement, I would urge Deaf Studies and Law departments within universities globally to create modules that explore deaf legal epistemologies. Legal academics should be encouraged to apply for research funding to develop projects that centre deaf legal experiences and frameworks. A specialist journal dedicated to Deaf Legal Studies would provide a much-needed focal point for publishing and shaping scholarship in this area. Conferences could also be convened to bring together scholars, lawyers, lawmakers, policymakers, interpreters, and activists, creating collaborative spaces for advancing research, policy and practice.

iii. Develop Deaf Jurisprudence

Jurisprudence is the philosophy or theory of law. It asks foundational questions about what law is, how it works, and how it should work. It provides the intellectual tools to examine legal structures, expose power dynamics, and challenge

[17] Michael Oliver, *Understanding Disability: From Theory to Practice*, 2nd edn (Palgrave Macmillan, 2009) 49.

[18] As a starting point, see 'Publications' (Deaf Legal Theory, 2025), https://deaflegaltheory.com/publications.

dominant assumptions. For decades, legal scholars have used feminist jurisprudence, Critical Race Theory, and Critical Disability Theory to reveal how the law marginalises certain groups. Deaf jurisprudence is the next step: a project that starts not from mainstream assumptions about law, but from deaf experiences, values, and ways of knowing.

At its heart, deaf jurisprudence asks: what would legal theory look like if it were grounded in deaf epistemologies? It challenges the idea that legal knowledge must always be expressed in spoken or written language, and instead embraces the visual, embodied, and collective modes of communication that define many deaf lives. It interrogates how legal systems frame deaf people: not just in terms of rights or access, but in terms of identity, capacity, culture, and language. And it explores how core legal concepts such as justice, participation, and equality might be reimagined if shaped from within deaf cultural frameworks.

Deaf Legal Theory provides the foundation for this work. As I argue, the law is not neutral: it is hearing. It reflects the assumptions, priorities and norms of a hearing majority, often requiring deaf people to misidentify themselves in order to be protected. Deaf Legal Theory exposes this systemic bias and offers a framework, grounded in critical legal studies, for analysing how the law frames deaf people, and how it might be reshaped.[19] Building on Deaf Legal Theory, developing deaf jurisprudence means creating space for deaf-led legal thought. This is a critical next step.

V. Conclusion

This book began with a provocation: that equality law does not work for deaf people. Not because of isolated policy failures, or poor implementation, but because the law itself is built on assumptions that do not reflect deaf lives. Across these chapters, I have explored how legal frameworks shape, constrain, and sometimes erase the experiences of deaf individuals. I have examined the concepts of equality, tested them through lived and imagined realities, and proposed alternative ways forward grounded in the values, practices, and epistemologies of deaf communities themselves.

What emerges is a pattern. Not of intentional exclusion, perhaps, but of structural misrecognition: of legal systems that expect deaf people to conform to categories they did not choose, and that rarely allow them to speak on their own terms. At the same time, there are possibilities. By shifting our framing, by rethinking legal concepts, reimagining deaf identity, and reworking how rights are understood, there are clear opportunities to build something better.

This book matters now because those opportunities are real, and the need is urgent. Legal reforms are being discussed. Sign languages are gaining visibility. But

[19] Rob Wilks, 'Deaf Legal Theory: Challenging the Law's Hearing Bias' (2025) 30 *Journal of Deaf Studies and Deaf Education* 293.

unless these developments are shaped by deaf people, and grounded in the realities of deaf experience, they risk repeating the same patterns in new forms.

Throughout this work, I have spoken from a dual position: as a legal scholar, and as a deaf person. That perspective has shaped the questions asked and the priorities identified. But this is not a singular account. It is an invitation: to think differently about law, about equality, and about the place of deaf people within both. The concepts I've introduced – the Deaf Legal Dilemma, Deaf Equality Concepts, and the Deaf Rights Model –are starting points. They are not definitive, but they are deliberate.

The work is unfinished, and that is as it should be. This is not a conclusion, but a continuation; one I hope others will take forward, challenge, adapt, and build upon. Deaf people deserve more than accommodation. They deserve recognition, respect, and full participation in the legal and political systems that shape their lives. This book sets out a path toward that goal. What happens next is up to all of us.

I reiterate: this book began with a simple provocation: equality law is audist. But over the course of this work, it has become clear it is not just equality law. The law as a whole is audist, in its design, its assumptions, its language and limits.

I end this book with both an invitation and a challenge: *what if it wasn't?*

BIBLIOGRAPHY

Acas, 'Reasonable Adjustments at Work: What Reasonable Adjustments Are' (30 January 2025), www.acas.org.uk/reasonable-adjustments.

Action on Hearing Loss, 'Working for Change 2018: Workplace Experiences - Survey Results' (2018).

Albertyn C and Goldblatt B, 'Facing the Challenge of Transformation: Difficulties in the Development of an Indigenous Jurisprudence of Equality' (1998) 14 *South African Journal on Human Rights* 248.

Alexiadou N, 'Social Inclusion and Social Exclusion in England: Tensions in Education Policy' (2002) 17 *Journal of Education Policy* 71.

Allen D, 'Rethinking the Australian Model of Promoting Gender Equality' in KG Young and K Rubenstein (eds), *The Public Law of Gender: From the Local to the Global* (Cambridge University Press, 2016).

Altman BM, 'Definitions, Models, Classifications, Schemes, and Applications' in G Albrecht, K Seelman and M Bury (eds), *Handbook of Disability Studies* (SAGE Publications, Inc, 2001), https://sk.sagepub.com/reference/hdbk_disability.

Andreevska E and Aziri E, 'Principle of Equality in International Law: The Right to Equality' (2009) 2 *Lex ET Scientia International Journal* 228.

Ardenne P d' and others, 'Does Interpreter-Mediated CBT with Traumatized Refugee People Work? A Comparison of Patient Outcomes in East London' (2007) 35 *Behavioural and Cognitive Psychotherapy* 293.

Arrowsmith L, 'Hidden Disadvantage' (2013), https://rnid.org.uk/wp-content/uploads/2020/05/Hidden-Disadvantage-full-report.pdf.

Association of Lipspeakers, 'Association of Lipspeakers (ALS): Spoken Words Made Visible' (2024), www.lipspeaking.co.uk.

Atkinson T, 'Social Inclusion and the European Union' (2002) 40 *Journal of Common Market Studies* 625.

Attfield K, 'The Deaf Collective: Opposition, Organisation and Difference' (Cardiff University, 2013).

Bamforth N, Malik M and O'Cinneide C, *Discrimination Law: Theory and Context, Text and Materials* (Sweet & Maxwell, 2008).

Barnard C, 'The Future of Equality Law: Equality and Beyond' in S Deakin, C Barnard and GS Morris (eds), *The Future of Labour Law. Liber Amicorum Sir Bob Hepple* (Hart Publishing, 2004).

Barnes L, 'Employment and Employability: The Experiences and Perceptions of Deaf Graduates' (Doctoral Thesis, University of Central Lancashire, 2017).

Bartolo L, '"Eyes Wide Open to the Context of Content": Reimagining the Hate Speech Policies of Social Media Platforms through a Substantive Equality Lens' (2021) 29 *Renewal: A Journal of Social Democracy* 39.

Barton L, *Disability and Society: Emerging Issues and Insights* (Longman, 1996).

Batterbury SC, 'Democratising Policy Theories: Enhancing Prospects for Language Justice for Sign Language Peoples' (2014) 42 *Policy & Politics* 547.

Batterbury-Magill S, 'The Legal Status of BSL and ISL' (2014), https://bda.org.uk/wp-content/uploads/2017/03/BDA_Legal-status-of-BSL-ISL_11-Mar-2014.pdf.

Bauman H-DL, 'Audism: Exploring the Metaphysics of Oppression' (2004) 9 *Journal of Deaf Studies and Deaf Education* 239.

Bell M, 'Judicial Enforcement of the Duties on Public Authorities to Promote Equality' [2010] *Public Law* 672.

Berger P, 'On the Obsolescence of the Concept of Honor' (1970) 11 *European Journal of Sociology* 339.

Blom H and others, 'Finding Friends Online: Online Activities by Deaf Students and Their Well-Being' (2014) 9 *PLoS ONE* e88351.
Bloxs A, 'The Deaf Duality Paradox as a Trait of the Deaf Legal Theory' in R Wilks and D O'Brien (eds), *Developing Deaf Legal Theory* (in preparation).
Borland J and others, 'Responding to Discrimination: The Geography and Geometry of Advice Provision in England, Scotland and Wales' (Equality and Human Rights Commission, 2009).
Bourn C and Whitmore J, *Anti-Discrimination Law in Britain* (Sweet & Maxwell, 1996).
Brennan M and Brown R, *Equality before the Law: Deaf People's Access to Justice* (Douglas McLean, 1997).
British Deaf Association, 'UN Committee Paves the Way for a BSL Act – British Deaf Association' (31 August 2017), https://bda.org.uk/press-release-uncrpd-bsl.
——, 'Position Statement on the Language Acquisition of Deaf Children' (2023), https://bda.org.uk/wp-content/uploads/2024/03/BDA-Early-Years-Position-Full-v1.docx.
——, 'BSL in Our Hands' (2025), https://bda.org.uk/bsl-in-our-hands.
——, 'What We Stand For' (2025), https://bda.org.uk/history/what-we-stand-for.
Broesterhuizen M, 'Faith in Deaf Culture' (2005) 66 *Theological Studies* 304.
BSL Curriculum Working Group, 'British Sign Language Curriculum for Primary and Secondary Schools', https://primarysite-prod-sorted.s3.amazonaws.com/frank-barnes-school-for-deaf-children/UploadedDocument/ce1d304c-f324-4223-9ed7-4d365a7c99bf/bsl-curriculum-final.pdf.
Burns A and Gupta DS, 'Reasonable Adjustments: The Way Forward' (2004) 154 *New Law Journal* 452.
Business Disability Forum, 'Reasonable Adjustments - What They Are and Why They Are Important' (11 September 2024), https://businessdisabilityforum.org.uk/resource/reasonable-adjustments-smes.
Butlin SF, 'The UN Convention on the Rights of Persons with Disabilities: Does the Equality Act 2010 Measure up to UK International Commitments?' (2011) 40 *Industrial Law Journal*.
Cano-Hila AB, 'Understanding Social Inclusion in Contemporary Society: Challenges, Reflections, Limitations, and Proposals' (2022) 10 *Social Inclusion* 1.
Christian BSL, 'Vocabulary, Prayers, Reflections, and Bible Passages in British Sign Language' (2025), https://christianbsl.com.
Church in Wales, 'Volume I: Prefatory Note' (2025), www.churchinwales.org.uk/en/clergy-and-members/constitution/volume-i-prefatory-note.
Clayton-Hathway K, 'The Public Sector Equality Duty - Analysis of Supporting Evidence' (Oxford Brookes Centre for Diversity Policy Research and Practice, 2013).
Clements L and Read J, 'The Dog That Didn't Bark: The Issue of Access under the European Convention on Human Rights by Disabled People' in A Lawson and C Gooding (eds), *Disability Rights in Europe: from theory to practice* (Hart Publishing, 2005).
Cole WM, 'Human Rights as Myth and Ceremony? Reevaluating the Effectiveness of Human Rights Treaties, 1981–2007 1' (2012) 117 *American Journal of Sociology* 1131.
Collins H, 'Discrimination, Equality and Social Inclusion' (2003) 66 *The Modern Law Review* 16.
Connolly M, *Townshend-Smith on Discrimination Law: Text, Cases and Materials* (Cavendish Publishing, 2004).
Consortium for Research in Deaf Education, '2022 UK-Wide Summary' (National Deaf Children's Society 2022), www.ndcs.org.uk/media/8489/cride-2022-uk-report-final.pdf.
Cordier R and others, 'A Systematic Review Evaluating the Psychometric Properties of Measures of Social Inclusion' (2017) 12 *PLOS ONE* e0179109.
Corker M, *Deaf and Disabled, or Deafness Disabled? Towards a Human Rights Perspective* (Open University Press, 1998).
Corntassel JJ and Primeau TH, 'The Paradox of Indigenous Identity: A Levels-of-Analysis Approach' (1998) 4 *Global Governance: A Review of Multilateralism and International Organizations* 139.
Cornwall A, 'Unpacking "Participation": Models, Meanings and Practices' (2008) 43 *Community Development Journal* 269.
Cotter DA and others, 'The Glass Ceiling Effect' (2001) 80 *Social Forces* 655.

Crenshaw K, 'Mapping the Margins: Intersectionality, Identity Politics, and Violence Against Women of Color' (1991) 43 *Stanford Law Review* 1241.

Crenshaw KW, 'Race, Reform, and Retrenchment: Transformation and Legitimation in Antidiscrimination Law' (1988) 101 *Harvard Law Review* 1331.

CRPD Committee, 'Inquiry Concerning the United Kingdom of Great Britain and Northern Ireland Carried out by the Committee under Article 6 of the Optional Protocol to the Convention: Report of the Committee' (2017) CRPD/C/15/4.

——, 'Follow up Table – Closed Cases', www.ohchr.org/sites/default/files/documents/hrbodies/crpd/FU-table-CRPD-cases.xlsx.

——, 'Table of Pending Cases', www.ohchr.org/sites/default/files/documents/hrbodies/crpd/2022-09-23/Table_pending_cases_CRPD.xlsx.

Cusack S and Pusey L, 'CEDAW and the Rights to Non-Discrimination and Equality' (2013) 14 *Melbourne Journal of International Law* 54.

Darwin C, 'The Public Sector Equality Duty: An Update and Overview' (GLD, 29 January 2016), www.matrixlaw.co.uk/wp-content/uploads/2016/03/27_01_2016_12_40_30_Public-Sector-Equality-Duty-Update-and-OverviewvP.pdf.

Davis LJ, *Enforcing Normalcy: Disability, Deafness, and the Body* (Verso, 1995).

——, 'Deafness and the Riddle of Identity' (*The Chronicle*, 12 January 2007), www.lennarddavis.com/downloads/deafnessandtheriddle.pdf.

De Meulder M, 'The Influence of Deaf People's Dual Category Status on Sign Language Planning: The British Sign Language (Scotland) Act (2015)' (2017) 18 *Current Issues in Language Planning* 215.

De Meulder M and Haualand H, 'Sign Language Interpreting Services: A Quick Fix for Inclusion?' (2019) 16 *Translation and Interpreting Studies* 19.

——, 'Sign Language Interpreting Services: A Quick Fix for Inclusion?' (World Association of Sign Language Interpreters Conference, Paris, France, 15 July 2019).

De Meulder M and Murray JJ, 'Buttering Their Bread on Both Sides?' (2017) 41 *Language Problems and Language Planning* 136.

Degener T, 'Disabled Persons and Human Rights: The Legal Framework' in T Degener and Y Koster-Dreese (eds), *Human Rights and Disabled Persons* (Kluwer Academic, 1995).

——, 'Disability in a Human Rights Context' (2016) 5 *Laws* 35.

——, 'A New Human Rights Model of Disability' in V Della Fina (ed), *The United Nations Convention on the Rights of Persons with Disabilities* (Springer, 2017).

Devlieger PJ, 'Generating a Cultural Model of Disability', 19th Congress of the European Federation of Associations of Teachers of the Deaf (2005), www.researchgate.net/profile/Patrick_Devlieger/publication/237762101_Generating_a_cultural_model_of_disability/links/5434004f0cf2dc341daf2bc1.pdf.

Dodenhoff P, 'Five Faces of Oppression - Disability Hate Crime in the UK' (*Disabled World*, 14 May 2014), www.disabled-world.com/disability/discrimination/faces.php.

Donnelly J, *Universal Human Rights in Theory and Practice* (Cornell University Press, 2013).

Dotson K, 'Conceptualizing Epistemic Oppression' (2014) 28 *Social Epistemology* 115.

Dunbar R, 'Language Legislation and Language Rights in the United Kingdom' (2002) 2 *European Yearbook of Minority Issues Online* 95.

Dworkin R, *Taking Rights Seriously* (Duckworth Press, 1977).

——, *A Matter of Principle* (Harvard University Press, 1985).

——, *Sovereign Virtue: The Theory and Practice of Equality* (Harvard University Press, 2000).

Eckert RC, 'Toward a Theory of Deaf Ethnos: Deafnicity ≈ D/Deaf (Homaemon – Homoglosson – Homothreskon)' (2010) 15 *Journal of Deaf Studies and Deaf Education* 317.

Eckert RC and Rowley AJ, 'Audism: A Theory and Practice of Audiocentric Privilege' (2013) 37 *Humanity & Society* 101.

Elkayam-Levy C, 'Re-Imagining the Rules - The Global Transition to Transformative Equality and the Narratives of Feminist Religious Movements' (2021), https://papers.ssrn.com/sol3/papers.cfm?abstract_id=3757963.

Emberton M, 'Unconscious Bias Is a Human Condition' (2021) 25 *The Permanente Journal* 1.
Emery SD, 'Citizenship and the Deaf Community' (Doctoral dissertation, University of Central Lancashire, 2006).
Emond A and others, 'The Current Health of the Signing Deaf Community in the UK Compared with the General Population: A Cross-Sectional Study.' (2015) 5 *BMJ Open* 1.
——, 'Access to Primary Care Affects the Health of Deaf People.' (2015) 65 *The British Journal of General Practice: the Journal of the Royal College of General Practitioners* 95.
Equal Rights Trust, 'The Ideas of Equality and Non-Discrimination, Formal and Substantive Equality' (2007), www.equalrightstrust.org/ertdocumentbank/The%20Ideas%20of%20Equality%20and%20Non-discrimination,%20Formal%20and%20Substantive%20Equality.pdf.
Equality and Human Rights Commission, 'UN Convention on the Rights of Persons with Disabilities' (21 January 2020), www.equalityhumanrights.com/en/our-human-rights-work/monitoring-and-promoting-un-treaties/un-convention-rights-persons-disabilities.
——, 'Technical Guidance on the Public Sector Equality Duty: England | EHRC' (2023), www.equalityhumanrights.com/guidance/public-sector-equality-duty/technical-guidance-public-sector-equality-duty-england-0#document-download.
Escobar A, 'Whose Knowledge, Whose Nature? Biodiversity, Conservation, and the Political Ecology of Social Movements' (1998) 5 *Journal of Political Ecology* 53.
European Court of Human Rights, 'Factsheet - Persons with Disabilities and the European Convention on Human Rights' (2024), www.echr.coe.int/documents/d/echr/FS_Disabled_ENG.
Evans E and Reher S, 'Barriers to Elected Office for Disabled People' (Government Equalities Office 2021), www.gov.uk/government/publications/barriers-to-elected-office-for-disabled-people/barriers-to-elected-office-for-disabled-people.
——, 'Disability and Political Representation: Analysing the Obstacles to Elected Office in the UK' (2022) 43 *International Political Science Review* 697.
Farid A and others, 'Negotiating Ideations: The Role of State-Led Identity-Making in the Progress of Women's Rights in Malaysia' (2022) 23 *Australian Journal of Asian Law* 9.
Felder F, Davy L and Kayess R (eds), *Disability Law and Human Rights: Theory and Policy* (Springer International Publishing, 2022).
Finkelstein V, 'Representing Disability' in John Swain and others (eds), *Disability Barriers – Enabling Environments* (SAGE Publications, 2004).
Flew A, 'Four Kinds of Equality' [1982] *Reason Papers* 17.
Fraser N, *Justice Interruptus: Critical Reflections on the 'Postsocialist' Condition* (Routledge, 1997).
——, 'From Redistribution to Recognition? Dilemmas of Justice in a "post-Socialist" Age' in JC Alexander and S Seidman (ed), *The New Social Theory Reader*, 2nd edn (Routledge, 2008).
Fredman S, 'Equality: A New Generation?' (2001) 30 *Industrial Law Journal* 145.
——, *Discrimination Law*, 1st edn (Oxford University Press, 2002).
——, 'The Future of Equality in Britain' (Equal Opportunities Commission, 2002).
——, 'Providing Equality: Substantive Equality and the Positive Duty to Provide' (2005) 21 *South African Journal on Human Rights* 163.
——, 'Substantive Equality Revisited' (2016) 14 *International Journal of Constitutional Law* 712.
——, 'Challenging the Frontiers of Gender Equality: Women at Work' in RJ Cook (ed), *Frontiers of Gender Equality* (University of Pennsylvania Press, 2023).
Fudge J, 'Substantive Equality, the Supreme Court of Canada, and the Limits to Redistribution 23: 235.' [2007] *South African Journal on Human Rights* 235.
Gaventa J, 'Finding the Spaces for Change: A Power Analysis' (2006) 37 23.
Gonsoulin TP, 'Cochlear Implant/Deaf World Dispute: Different Bottom Elephants' 125 *Otolaryngology – Head and Neck Surgery* 552.
Goonesekere SWE, 'The Indivisibility of Rights and Substantive Equality for Women' in N Reilly (ed), *International Human Rights of Women* (Springer Singapore, 2019).
GOV.UK, 'Tribunals Statistics Quarterly: July to September 2023' (14 December 2023), www.gov.uk/government/statistics/tribunals-statistics-quarterly-july-to-september-2023.

——, 'Disability Confident Employer Scheme' (24 April 2024), www.gov.uk/government/collections/disability-confident-campaign.
——, 'Civil Justice Statistics Quarterly: October to December 2024' (6 March 2025), www.gov.uk/government/statistics/civil-justice-statistics-quarterly-october-to-december-2024.
——, 'Tribunals Statistics Quarterly: October to December 2024' (13 March 2025),www.gov.uk/government/statistics/tribunals-statistics-quarterly-october-to-december-2024.
Grabham E, 'Law v Canada: New Directions for Equality Under the Canadian Charter?' (2002) 22 *Oxford Journal of Legal Studies* 641.
Grant E, 'Dignity and Equality' (2007) 7 *a* 299.
Greschner D, 'Does Law Advance the Cause of Equality' [2001] *Queen's Law Journal* 99.
Gulliver M, 'Places of Silence' in F Vanclay, M Higgins and A Blackshaw (eds), *Making Sense of Place* (National Museum of Australia Press, 2008).
——, 'Practice of Religion by Deaf People' (14 May 2018).
Hadjikakou K and Nikolaraizi M, 'Deaf Clubs Today: Do They Still Have a Role to Play? The Cases of Cyprus and Greece' (2011) 155 *American Annals of the Deaf* 605.
Hahn H, 'Antidiscrimination Laws and Social Research on Disability: The Minority Group Perspective' (1996) 14 *Behavioral Sciences & the Law* 41.
Harpur P and Douglas H, 'Disability and Domestic Violence: Protecting Survivors' Human Rights' (2015) 23 *Griffith Law Review* 405.
Harrington F and Turner GH, *Interpreting Interpreting: Studies and Reflections on Sign Language Interpreting* (Douglas McLean, 2000).
Hastrup K and Fog Olwig K (eds), *Siting Culture: The Shifting Anthropological Object* (Routledge, 1997).
Hay G, O'Neill R, and Wilks R, 'Scotland, BSL, Language Recognition and the Law' (Deaf Studies Conference, University of Wolverhampton, February 2019).
Helfer LR, 'Consensus, Coherence and the European Convention' (1993) 26 *Cornell International Law Journal* 133.
Hellman D and Moreau S, *Philosophical Foundations of Discrimination Law* (Oxford University Press, 2015).
Hendriks A and Degener T, 'The Evolution of a European Perspective on Disability Legislation' (1994) 1 *European Journal of Health Law* 343.
Hepple B, 'The Aims of Equality Law' (2008) 61 *Current Legal Problems* 1.
——, 'The New Single Equality Act in Britain' (2010) 5 *Equal Rights Review* 11.
——, 'Enforcing Equality Law: Two Steps Forward and Two Steps Backwards for Reflexive Regulation' (2011) 40 *Industrial Law Journal* 315.
——, 'Transformative Equality: The Role of Democratic Participation' (Labour Law Research Network Inaugural Conference, 13–15 June 2013, Pompeu Fabra University, Barcelona, 2013).
——, *Equality: The Legal Framework*, 2nd edn (Hart Publishing, 2014).
Hernández González J, 'Applying the Five Faces of Oppression to Climate Justice: Analysing Discussions of Climate Justice with the Help of Iris Marion Young's Theory of Oppression' (Master's Dissertation, Utrecht University, 2021), https://studenttheses.uu.nl/bitstream/handle/20.500.12932/40655/Thesis%205936381%202_06_2021%20%281%29.pdf?sequence=1&isAllowed=y.
Hodson L, 'Gender and the International Judge: Towards a Transformative Equality Approach' (2022) 35 *Leiden Journal of International Law* 913.
Holmes E, 'Anti-Discrimination Rights Without Equality' (2005) 68 *The Modern Law Review* 175.
House of Lords Select Committee on the Equality Act 2010 and Disability, 'The Equality Act 2010: The Impact on Disabled People' (Stationery Office Limited, 2016) HL Paper 117, https://publications.parliament.uk/pa/ld201516/ldselect/ldeqact/117/117.pdf.
Hulme C, Young A and Munro KJ, 'Exploring the Lived Experiences of British Sign Language (BSL) Users Who Access NHS Adult Hearing Aid Clinics: An Interpretative Phenomenological Analysis' (2022) 61 *International Journal of Audiology* 744.
Humphries T, 'Communicating across Cultures (Deaf-Hearing) and Language Learning' (Doctoral Thesis, Union Institute and University, 1977).

——, 'Of Deaf-Mutes, the Strange, and the Modern Deaf Self' in M Harvey and N Glickman (eds), *Culturally Affirming Psychotherapy with Deaf Persons* (Lawrence Erlbaum Associates, 1996).
——, 'The Right to Language' (2014) 41 *The Journal of Law, Medicine & Ethics* 872.
Hunt R, Oram R and Young A, 'Older People Who Use BSL – Preferences for Residential Care Provision in Wales' (University of Manchester, 2010), https://apps.mhs.manchester.ac.uk/uploads/ProjectProfilesFiles/2184/OlderPeopleWalesOctoberFinalrevised.pdf.
Hurst R, 'Legislation and Human Rights' in J Swain and others (eds), *Disability Barriers – Enabling Environments* (SAGE Publications, 2004).
International Labour Organization, 'Indigenous and Tribal Peoples Convention' (1989) No 169, https://normlex.ilo.org/dyn/nrmlx_en/f?p=NORMLEXPUB:12100:0::NO::P12100_ILO_CODE:C169.
Jewish Deaf Association, *Sign Language in Judaism* (2003).
Katiyatiya LM and Lubisi N, 'Part B: The Role of Substantive Equality in Shaping Transformative Social Protection in South Africa into the Digital Platform Work' (2021) 25 *Journal of Poverty* 23.
Keith LC, 'The United Nations International Covenant on Civil and Political Rights: Does It Make a Difference in Human Rights Behavior?' (1999) 36 *Journal of Peace Research* 95.
Kelly L, 'Suffering in Silence: The Unmet Needs of d/Deaf Prisoners' [2017] *Prison Service Journal* 3.
Kelly LM, 'Sounding out d/Deafness: The Experiences of d/Deaf Prisoners' (2017) 8 *Journal of Criminal Psychology* 20.
Kelly-Corless L and McCulloch D, 'Why Deaf Prisoners Have Been in a State of Lockdown since Well before COVID-19' (*The Conversation*, 13 April 2021), https://theconversation.com/why-deaf-prisoners-have-been-in-a-state-of-lockdown-since-well-before-covid-19-158173.
Khaitan T, *A Theory of Discrimination Law* (Oxford University Press, 2014).
Killian LM, 'What or Who Is a "Minority"?' [1996] *Michigan Sociological Review* 18.
Kingsbury B, 'Self-Determination and "Indigenous Peoples"' (1992) 86 *American Society of International Law Proceedings* 383.
Knight P, 'Deafness and Disability' in S Gregory and others (eds), *Issues in Deaf Education* (David Fulton Publishers, 1998).
Koller D, Pouesard ML and Rummens JA, 'Defining Social Inclusion for Children with Disabilities: A Critical Literature Review' (2018) 32 *Children & Society* 1.
Krausneker V, 'Has Something Changed? Sign Languages in Europe: The Case of Minorised Minority Languages' (2003) 19 *Deaf Worlds: International Journal of Deaf Studies* 33.
Kusters A, 'Deaf Utopias? Reviewing the Sociocultural Literature on the World's "Martha's Vineyard Situations"' (2010) 15 *Journal of Deaf Studies and Deaf Education* 3.
Kyle J, Sutherland H and Stockley S, 'Legal Choice - Silent Process: Engaging Legal Services When You Do Not Hear' (Deaf Studies Trust, 2012).
Ladd P, *Understanding Deaf Culture: In Search of Deafhood* (Multilingual Matters, 2003).
Ladd P and Lane HL, 'Deaf Ethnicity, Deafhood, and Their Relationship' (2013) 13 *Sign Language Studies* 56.
Ladd P and Woll B, 'Deaf Communities' in M Marschark and PE Spencer (eds), *The Oxford Handbook of Deaf Studies, Language, and Education*, vol 1, 2nd edn (Oxford University Press, 2011).
Lambert M, 'Austerity Has Trampled over Disabled People's Rights. But the UK Won't Admit It' (*The Guardian*, 4 September 2017), www.theguardian.com/commentisfree/2017/sep/04/austerity-disabled-people-rights-uk-un-government.
Lane H, *The Mask of Benevolence: Disabling the Deaf Community* (Alfred A Knopf, 1992).
Lane HL, 'Do Deaf People Have a Disability?' (2002) 2 *Sign Language Studies* 356.
Lane HL, Hoffmeister R and Bahan B, *A Journey into the Deaf-World* (DawnSignPress, 1996).
Lane HL, Pillard RC, and Hedberg U, *People of the Eye: Deaf Ethnicity and Ancestry* (Oxford University Press, 2010).
Lawson A, 'The EU Rights Based Approach to Disability: Strategies for Shaping an Inclusive Society' (2005) 6 *International Journal of Discrimination and the Law* 269.
Lawson J, 'Disability as a Cultural Identity' (2001) 11 *International Studies in Sociology of Education* 203.
Levitas R, *The Inclusive Society?: Social Exclusion and New Labour*, 2nd edn (Palgrave Macmillan, 2005).

——, 'The Multidimensional Analysis of Social Exclusion' (University of Bristol, 2007), https://dera.ioe.ac.uk/id/eprint/6853/1/multidimensional.pdf.

Lexis+ UK Practical Guidance, 'Practice Note - Public Sector Equality Duty', https://plus.lexis.com/uk/practical-guidance-uk/public-sector-equality-duty.

Liao S and and Carbonell V, 'Materialized Oppression in Medical Tools and Technologies' (2023) 23 *The American Journal of Bioethics* 9.

Liisberg MV, *Disability and Employment: A Contemporary Disability Human Rights Approach Applied to Danish, Swedish and EU Law and Policy* (Intersentia, 2011).

Lundeberg IR and Breivik J-K, 'Being Deaf in Court' (2015) 17 *Scandinavian Journal of Disability Research* 42.

Lyons WJ, 'The Story of John P. Gloyn and "The City Road Congregation" (1872-1877), or How a Deaf-Led Deaf Space Came into Existence in Victorian North London' (2024) 21 *Cultural and Social History* 41.

M Gordon, *The Scope of Sociology* (Oxford University Press, 1988).

Maiorana-Basas M and Pagliaro CM, 'Technology Use Among Adults Who Are Deaf and Hard of Hearing: A National Survey' (2014) 19 *The Journal of Deaf Studies and Deaf Education* 400.

Manfredi S, Vickers L and Clayton-Hathway K, 'The Public Sector Equality Duty: Enforcing Equality Rights Through Second-Generation Regulation' (2018) 47 *Industrial Law Journal* 365.

Marko J, 'Against Discrimination' in J Marko and S Constantin (eds), *Human and Minority Rights Protection by Multiple Diversity Governance*, 1st edn (Routledge, 2019).

Martin C, 'Culturo-Linguistic Congruity in the Residential Care of the Elderly and Cognitively Impaired in North Wales' (MRes Dissertation, Bangor University, 2021).

Martínez Cobo JR, 'Study of the Problem of Discrimination Against Indigenous Populations' (United Nations 1986) E/CN.4/Sub.2/1986/7/Add.4.

McColgan A, *Discrimination Law: Text, Cases and Materials* (Hart Publishing, 2005).

——, 'Cracking the Comparator Problem: Discrimination, "Equal" Treatment and the Role of Comparisons' [2006] *European Human Rights Law Review* 650.

——, *Human Rights Law in Perspective: Discrimination, Equality and the Law* (Bloomsbury, 2014).

McCrudden C, 'Merit Principles' (1998) 18 *Oxford Journal of Legal Studies* 543.

McCulloch D, 'Not Hearing Us: An Exploration of the Experience of Deaf Prisoners in English and Welsh Prisons' (Howard League for Penal Reform, 2012), http://oro.open.ac.uk/42456.

McGonigle Leyh B and Fraser J, 'Transformative Reparations: Changing the Game or More of the Same?' (2019) 8 *Cambridge International Law Journal* 39.

McGregor J and Davies SG, 'Achieving Pay Equity: Strategic Mobilization for Substantive Equality in Aotearoa New Zealand' (2019) 26 *Gender, Work & Organization* 619.

McIlroy G and Storbeck C, 'Development of Deaf Identity: An Ethnographic Study' (2011) 16 *Journal of Deaf Studies and Deaf Education* 494.

McKee MM and Hauser PC, 'Juggling Two Worlds' in DF Moores and PV Paul (ed), *Deaf Epistemologies: Multiple Perspectives on the Acquisition of Knowledge* (Gallaudet University Press, 2012).

McKeown M, 'Structural Injustice' (2021) 16 *Philosophy Compass* e12757.

McLachlin BM, 'Equality, the Most Difficult Right' (2001) 14 *The Supreme Court Law Review: Osgoode's Annual Constitutional Cases Conference* 17.

McLeod W, 'Securing the Status of Gaelic? Implementing the Gaelic Language (Scotland) Act 2005' [2006] *Scottish Affairs* 19.

Meager N and others, 'Costs and Benefits to Service Providers of Making Reasonable Adjustments under Part III of the Disability Discrimination Act' (Institute for Employment Studies 2002) Research Report No 169, www.researchgate.net/profile/Nigel_Meager/publication/269101724_Costs_and_benefits_to_service_providers_of_making_reasonable_adjustments_under_Part_III_of_the_Disability_Discrimination_Act/links/5480652f0cf25b80dd71f6c2.pdf.

Monaghan K, *Blackstone's Guide to the Disability Discrimination Legislation* (Oxford University Press, 2005).

Moreau SR, 'The Wrongs of Unequal Treatment' (2004) 54 *University of Toronto Law Journal* 291.

Morris W, *Theology without Words: Theology in the Deaf Community* (Routledge, 2009).
Muehlebach A, '"Making Place" at the United Nations: Indigenous Cultural Politics at the U.N. Working Group on Indigenous Populations' (2001) 16 *Cultural Anthropology* 415.
Muhlke A-M, 'The Right to Language and Linguistic Development: Deafness from a Human Rights Perspective' (2000) 40 *Virginia Journal of International Law* 705.
Myers LL and Thyer BA, 'Social Work Practice with Deaf Clients: Issues in Culturally Competent Assessment' (1997) 26 *Social Work in Health Care* 61.
National Deaf Children's Society, 'Deaf Pupils Achieve an Entire GCSE Grade Less for Sixth Year Running' (9 August 2021), www.ndcs.org.uk/about-us/news-and-media/latest-news/deaf-pupils-achieve-an-entire-gcse-grade-less-for-sixth-year-running.
O'Brien D, Stead L and Nourse N, 'Bristol Deaf Memories: Archives, Nostalgia and the Loss of Community Space in the Deaf Community in Bristol' (2019) 20 899.
O'Brien N, 'Postliberal Accountability: The Challenge of Disability Human Rights' in *Politics and Administrative Justice: Postliberalism, Street-Level Bureaucracy and the Reawakening of Democratic Citizenship* (Bristol University Press, 2023).
O'Cinneide C, 'Beyond the Limits of Equal Treatment: The Use of Positive Duties in Equality Law' (Mainstreaming Equality: Models for a Statutory Duty, Equality Authority, Dublin, Ireland, 27 February 2003).
——, 'Fumbling Towards Coherence: The Slow Evolution of Equality and Anti-Discrimination Law in Britain' (2006) 57 *Northern Ireland Legal Quarterly* 57.
——, 'Equality: Current and Future Directions of Travel' (The Equality Act 2010: five-years on conference, Chester, June 2015).
——, 'Equality, Rights and the "Stickiness" of the Current Political Moment' in K Arabadjieva and others (eds), *Transformative Ideas – Ensuring a Just Share of Progress for All* (ETUI aisbl, 2023).
O'Dell L, 'Deaf News: Deaf Local Election Candidate "Denied" Interpreter Funding by Government' (*Limping Chicken*, 16 April 2021), https://limpingchicken.com/2021/04/16/deaf-news-deaf-local-election-candidate-denied-interpreter-funding-by-government.
Office of the High Commissioner for Human Rights, 'Committee on the Rights of Persons with Disabilities Reviews Report of the United Kingdom: Country Review' (24 August 2017), www.ohchr.org/en/press-releases/2017/08/committee-rights-persons-disabilities-reviews-report-united-kingdom.
Oliver M, *Understanding Disability: From Theory to Practice*, 2nd edn (Palgrave Macmillan, 2009).
Oliver M and Barnes C, *The New Politics of Disablement* (Palgrave Macmillan, 2012).
O'Neill R and others, 'Families Living on a Low Income Bringing up Deaf Children' (2019), www.ssc.education.ed.ac.uk/research/tellingit/tellingit_final.pdf.
Oxoby R, 'Understanding Social Inclusion, Social Cohesion, and Social Capital' (2009) 36 *International Journal of Social Economics* 1133.
Pabsch A, 'Lessons from the 2013 EUD UNCRPD Survey' in A Pabsch (ed), *Article 29: Participation in Political and Public Life* (European Union of the Deaf, 2014).
Padden C and Humphries T, *Deaf in America: Voices from a Culture* (Harvard University Press, 1990).
Panaccio C-M, '*Apologia* for a General Doctrine of Substantive Equality and Discrimination' (2020) 11 *Jurisprudence* 213.
Pandey P, 'Analysis of the Australian Federal and Victorian Anti-Discrimination Legislation in Achieving the Public Policy Goal of Substantive Equality' (2022) 7 *NUJS Journal of Regulatory Studies* 1.
Patrick D, 'Indigenous Contexts' in M Martin-Jones, A Blackledge and A Creese (eds), *The Routledge Handbook of Multilingualism* (Routledge, 2012).
Peters MA and Besley TAC, 'Social Exclusion/Inclusion: Foucault's Analytics of Exclusion, the Political Ecology of Social Inclusion and the Legitimation of Inclusive Education' (2014) 1 *Open Review of Educational Research* 99.
Phillips A, 'Defending Equality of Outcome' [2004] *Journal of Political Philosophy* 1.
Pring J, 'Government Faces Legal Action over Election Access Fund' (*Disability News Service*, 12 April 2018), www.disabilitynewsservice.com/government-faces-legal-action-over-election-access-fund.

Purdam K and others, 'Disability in the UK: Measuring Equality' (2008) 23 *Disability & Society* 53.
Quinn G and others, 'Human Rights and Disability: The Current Use and Future Potential of United Nations Human Rights Instruments in the Context of Disability' (United Nations Press, 2002).
Reaume DG, 'Discrimination and Dignity' (2003) 63 *Louisiana Law Review* 645.
Ribot JC and Peluso NL, 'A Theory of Access' (2003) 68 *Rural Sociology* 153.
Robinson O, 'Puppets, Jesters, Memes, and Benevolence Porn: The Spectacle of Access' [2022] *Przegląd Kulturoznawczy* 329.
Roemer JE, *Equality of Opportunity* (Harvard University Press, 1998).
Rosdianti Y, 'Vindicating Substantive Equality in the Right to Work of Persons with Disabilities in Indonesia' (Doctoral Dissertation, National University of Ireland Galway, 2019).
Rowley K, 'Language Acquisition: Bimodal and Bilingual' (BDA BSL Conference, London, 17 March 2023), https://vimeo.com/812803921.
Royal Association for Deaf people, 'Deaf Advance: Deaf People, Employment and Career Progression' (2021).
Royal National Institute for Deaf People, 'The Equality Act 2010' (16 March 2021), https://rnid.org.uk/information-and-support/your-rights/the-equality-act-2010.
Royal National Institute for Deaf People and SignHealth, 'Still Ignored: The Fight for Accessible Healthcare - 2025 Research Report' (2025), https://signhealth.org.uk/wp-content/uploads/2025/04/ENGLAND-Still-Ignored-The-fight-for-Accessible-Healthcare-RESEARCH-report-FINAL.pdf.
RuleofLawInstitutePerson, 'Deaf Jurors and Discrimination' (Rule of Law Education Centre, 14 June 2016), www.ruleoflaw.org.au/deaf-jurors-and-discrimination.
Sabatello M, 'Disability, Cultural Minorities, and International Law: Reconsidering the Case of the Deaf Community' (2005) 26 1025.
Satish S, 'The World Bank Policy on Indigenous Peoples' (South Asia Sector Social Development 1999), https://documents1.worldbank.org/curated/en/535811468771538686/pdf/30438.pdf.
Schaar J, 'Equality of Opportunity, and Beyond' in JW Chapman and J Roland Pennock (eds), *Equality* (Atherton Press, 1967).
Schermerhorn RA, *Comparative Ethnic Relations: A Framework for Theory and Research* (University of Chicago Press, 1978).
Schiek D, Waddington L and Bell M, *Cases, Materials and Text on National, Supranational and International Non-Discrimination Law* (Hart Publishing, 2007).
Sclater E, 'Making Practice Happen: Practitioners' Views on the Most Effective Specific Equality Duties' (Equality and Human Rights Commission 2009), www.edf.org.uk/wp-content/uploads/2009/02/final-report-making-practice-happen.pdf.
Scotch RK, 'Disability as the Basis for a Social Movement: Advocacy and the Politics of Definition' (1988) 44 *Journal of Social Issues* 159.
Shakespeare T, *Disability Rights and Wrongs* (Routledge, 2006).
Shared Intelligence, 'Evaluation of the Equality Delivery System for the NHS - Phase One: Final Report' (University Hospitals Birmingham NHS Foundation Trust, 2012), www.uhb.nhs.uk/Downloads/pdf/EdsEvaluationPhaseOneFinalReport.pdf.
SignHealth, 'How the Health Service Is Failing Deaf People' (SignHealth, 2014).
Sinha V and others, 'Substantive Equality and Jordan's Principle: Challenges and Complexities' (2021) 35 *Journal of Law and Social Policy* 21.
Singh S, 'Conceptualising "Black Lives Matter": Time to Consider Substantive Equality as a Fundamental Constitutional Guarantee' (2021) 16 *Amity Law Review* 70.
Sreenivasan G, 'Equality, Opportunity, Ambiguity' (2014) 13 *Politics, Philosophy & Economics* 82.
St John's Deaf Community Centre, 'About' (2023), https://sites.google.com/sjdcc.org.uk/stjohnsdeafcommunitycentre/noticeboards/About.
Sutton-Spence R and Kaneko M, *Introducing Sign Language Literature: Folklore and Creativity* (Red Globe Press, 2016).

Swain J, 'International Perspectives on Disability' in J Swain and others (eds), *Disability Barriers – Enabling Environments* (SAGE Publications, 2004).

Swinbourne C, 'Bristol's Deaf Community Feel under Siege' (*The Guardian*, 15 September 2011), www.theguardian.com/commentisfree/2011/sep/15/bristol-deaf-centre-funding-cuts.

Tajfel H, 'Experiments in Intergroup Discrimination' (1970) 223 *Scientific American* 96.

Terry J and others, 'Deaf People Wales: Hidden Inequality' (2021), www.swansea.ac.uk/media/Deaf-People-Wales_Hidden-Inequality-2021.pdf.

Thibodeau R, 'Dynamics of Deaf Leadership: A Theoretical Model' (Doctoral dissertation, University of Southern Maine, 2019).

Thornton M, 'Domesticating Disability Discrimination' (1997) 2 *International Journal of Discrimination and the Law* 183.

——, 'Equality and Anti-Discrimination Legislation: An Uneasy Relationship' (2021) 37 *Law in Context* 12.

Totaljobs, 'Deaf Jobseeker and Employee Experiences Survey' (2016), www.121captions.com/wp-content/uploads/2017/08/Deaf-jobseeker-and-employee-experiences-survey-report-2016.pdf.

UK Government, 'The UK's 2022 Follow-up Report to the 2016 Inquiry by the UN Committee on the Rights of Persons with Disabilities' (2022), https://assets.publishing.service.gov.uk/media/639b0a96e90e072182dffe8f/FINAL_Web-Accessible_UK_2022_follow-up_inquiry_report_UNCRPD.pdf.

UK Parliament, 'Chapter 12: Participation in Politics' (*Select Committee on the Equality Act 2010 and Disability The Equality Act 2010: the impact on disabled people*, 24 March 2016), https://publications.parliament.uk/pa/ld201516/ldselect/ldeqact/117/11715.htm.

Union of the Physically Impaired Against Segregation and Disability Alliance, 'Fundamental Principles of Disability', https://disability-studies.leeds.ac.uk/wp-content/uploads/sites/40/library/UPIAS-fundamental-principles.pdf.

United Nations, 'Consideration of Reports Submitted by States Parties under Article 35 of the Convention. Initial Reports of States Parties Due in 2011: United Kingdom of Great Britain and Northern Ireland' (CRPD Committee, 2011) UN Doc CRPD/C/GBR/1.

——, 'Australia Violated Rights of Deaf People over Jury Service – UN Experts' (Office of the High Commissioner for Human Rights, 26 April 2016), www.ohchr.org/en/press-releases/2016/04/australia-violated-rights-deaf-people-over-jury-service-un-experts.

——, 'Rules of Procedure' (CRPD Committee 2016) UN Doc CRPD/C/1/Rev.1

——, 'Individual Communications' (Office of the High Commissioner for Human Rights, 2025), www.ohchr.org/en/treaty-bodies/individual-communications.

Valentine G and Skelton T, 'Changing Spaces: The Role of the Internet in Shaping Deaf Geographies' (2008) 9 *Social & Cultural Geography* 469.

——, '"An Umbilical Cord to the World": The Role of the Internet in D/Deaf People's Information and Communication Practices' (2009) 12 *Information, Communication & Society* 44.

Vargas C and others, 'Co-Creation, Co-Design, Co-Production for Public Health – a Perspective on Definition and Distinctions' (2022) 32 *Public Health Research & Practice* 1.

Vernon A, Barnes V, and Mercer G, 'Reflexivity: The Dilemmas of Researching from the Inside' *Doing Disability Research* (The Disability Press, 1997).

Vickers L, 'Promoting Equality or Fostering Resentment? The Public Sector Equality Duty and Religion and Belief' (2011) 31 *Legal Studies* 135.

Waddington L and Lawson A, 'Disability and Non-Discrimination Law in the European Union' (European Commission 2009), https://publications.europa.eu/en/publication-detail/-/publication/cf7bc8c8-2c84-46ff-83b5-202a6fb805a1.

Wadham J and others (eds), *Blackstone's Guide to the Equality Act 2010*, 3rd edn (Oxford University Press, 2016).

Watkins K and Marsick V, *Informal and Incidental Learning in the Workplace* (Routledge, 1990).

Wells K, 'The Impact of the Framework Employment Directive on UK Disability Discrimination Law' (2003) 32 *Industrial Law Journal* 253.

Westen P, 'The Empty Idea of Equality' (1982) 95 *Harvard Law Review* 537.
——, *Speaking of Equality: An Analysis of the Rhetorical Force of Equality in Moral and Legal Discourse* (Princeton University Press, 1990).
White R and others, 'Court Accommodations for Persons with Severe Communication Disabilities: A Legal Scoping Review' (2021) 27 *Psychology, Public Policy, and Law* 399.
Whittle R, 'The Framework Directive for Equal Treatment in Employment and Occupation: An Analysis from a Disability Rights Perspective' (2002) 27 *European Law Review* 303.
Wilks R, 'Developing Deaf Jurisprudence: The Role of Interpreters and Translators' in C Stone and others (eds), *Routledge Handbook of Sign Language Translation and Interpreting* (Routledge, 2022).
——, 'Deaf Legal Theory: Challenging the Law's Hearing Bias' (2025) 30 *Journal of Deaf Studies and Deaf Education* 293.
——, 'From Barking Dogs to Roarless Dragons: The Legal Recognition of British Sign Language across the United Kingdom' [in press] *Sign Language Studies*.
Wilks R and Brattan-Wilson J, 'Making the Law Work for Young Deaf People' (Royal Association for Deaf People, 2012).
Wilks R and O'Neill R, 'Deaf Education in Scotland and Wales: Attitudes to British Sign Language in Deaf Education Compared to Gaelic and Welsh' (2022), https://blogs.ed.ac.uk/deafeducation/wp-content/uploads/sites/5764/2022/10/2-FINAL-REPORT.pdf.
——, 'Integrating British Sign Language into Deaf Education' [submitted] *The Language Learning Journal*.
Wilks R and Venade De Sousa F, 'Interpreting the European Charter for Regional and Minority Languages: Sign Languages as Regional and Minority Languages' (2025) 32 *The International Journal of Speech, Language and the Law* 62.
Wilks RB, 'Making Equality Law Work for Deaf People' (Doctoral Dissertation, University of Leicester, 2019).
Wilks, R, 'Special Section: Introducing Deaf Legal Studies - Editorial' (2026) 7(2) *Amicus Curiae*.
Wox L, 'A Deaf Child's Right to Language: A Human Rights Approach to Language Law and Policy to Eradicate Language Deprivation' (University of the West of England Bristol, in progress).
Wu, C and Grant Nancy NC, 'Intersectionality—Beyond the Individual: A Look Into Cultural Identity Development of Deaf and Hard-of-Hearing Children of Multicultural "Hearing" Families' in IW Leigh and CA O'Brien (eds), *Deaf Identities: Exploring New Frontiers* (Oxford University Press, 2019).
Young A, 'Older Deaf People and Social Care: A Review' (Royal Association for Deaf People and [sonus] 2014), https://research.manchester.ac.uk/files/67726760/POST-PEER-REVIEW-PUBLISHERS.PDF.
Young IM, *Justice and the Politics of Difference* (Princeton University Press, 1990).
——, 'Status Inequality and Social Groups' (2002) 2 *Issues in Legal Scholarship* [i].

INDEX

www.ingramcontent.com/pod-product-compliance
Ingram Content Group UK Ltd.
Pitfield, Milton Keynes, MK11 3LW, UK
UKHW020821290926
15470UKWH00003B/1300